Years of Fire and Ash
South African Poems of Decolonisation

years of fire and ash

edited by Wamuwi Mbao

south african poems of decolonisation

Ad Donker Publishers
Johannesburg • Cape Town • London

All rights reserved. No part of this publication may be reproduced, stored in a retrieval system, or transmitted, in any form or by any means, electronic, mechanical, photocopying, or otherwise, without prior permission from the publisher or copyright holder.

© This selection, Wamuwi Mbao 2021
© The copyright for each individual poem remains with the poet

© Published by AD DONKER PUBLISHERS, 2021
An imprint of Jonathan Ball Publishers
A division of Media24 (Pty) Limited
PO Box 33977
Jeppestown
2043

ISBN 978-0-86852-251-7

The poems on pages 25 – 111 originally appeared in Michael Chapman and Achmat Dangor's *Voices From Within: Black Poetry from Southern Africa* (Ad Donker, 1982). Sindiswa Busuku's poem 'Midnight in Lusikisiki' originally appeared in *Pride and Prejudice: The Gerald Kraak Anthology: African Perspectives on Gender, Social Justice and Sexuality* (Jacana 2017). Maneo Mohale's poem 'Letsatsi' originally appeared in *Everything Is A Deathly Flower* (uHlanga, 2019).

www.jonathanball.co.za
www.twitter.com/JonathanBallPub
www.facebook.com/JonathanBallPublishers

Cover, design and typesetting by Michiel Botha

Contents

Introduction 9

Pre-Sharpeville (1890–1960)
Africa: My Native Land – Mrs AC Dube   25
'Civilised' Labour Policy – lr   26
The Making of a Servant – JJR Jolobe   27
The Gold Mines – BW Vilakazi   30
Freedom's Child – Peter Abrahams   36
Because I'm Black – HIE Dhlomo   40

Post-Sharpeville (1960–1976)
Always a Suspect – Mbuyiseni Oswald Mtshali   43
The Pension Jiveass – Mandlenkosi Langa   44
The Miners – Mafika Mbuli   45
Kneel and Pray – Nkathazo ka Mnyayiza   47
The Man of Smoke – Njabulo S Ndebele   48
Location Fires – Jennifer Davids   52
What's in this Black 'Shit' – Mongane Wally Serote   53
Getting off the Ride – Mafika Gwala   55

Post-Soweto (1976–)

the morning caught me – Shabbir Banoobhai 67
thinking about a white christmas – Fhazel Johennesse 68
The Dying Ground – Monnapule Lebakeng 69
from: black trial – Ingoapele Madingoane 71
The Question – Themba ka Miya 78
Soul's Disparity – Motlase Mogotsi 82
Old Homes – David Moja-Mphuso 83
Our Immortal Mother – Molahlehi wa Mmutle 84
Death – Es'kia Mphahlele 86
Nineteen Seventy-Six – Oupa Thando Mthimkulu 90
Ngwana wa Azania – Mothobi Mutloatse 91
In this World, my Sister – Nthambeleni Phalanndwa 96
My Name – Magoleng wa Selepe 104
We the Dancers – Eugene Skeef 105
Custodian of our Spirit – Farouk Stemmet 107
Wooden Spoon – K Zwide 109
A Riot Policeman – Christopher van Wyk 110

Present Day

john 1:1 and me – Lebohang Masango 115
clots of blood – Vangile Gantsho 118
Black Beauty – Katleho Kano Shoro 120
born(e) to the grave – Mjele Msimang 121
jol'iinkomo – David wa Maahlamela 124
Citizen Minus – Khadija Heeger 130
A love poem to the 'Problematic' Black Womxn –
    Puleng Lange Stewart 133
Your Poem Saved Me – Ayanda Billie 138
Untitled poem #1 – Ashanti Kunene 139
Izint'eziphukile / Broken things – Siza Nkosi Mokhele 140
#FeesMustFall – Zéwande Bk. Bhengu 144

The Forgotten – Sithembiso 'Sthe Khali' Khalishwayo   146
Midnight in Lusikisiki (or The Ruin of the Gentlewomen) –
   Sindiswa Busuku   152
Crowd Gathered, Salivating for a Taste of Blood –
   Sihle Ntuli   153
Letsatsi – Maneo Mohale   154
Blvcksuburbia – Anga Mamfanya   156
History in my Body – Uhuru Phalafala   158
The ocean seeks revenge – Sibongile Fisher   161
fatigue of revolution – Masai Sepuru   163

Index of poems   167
Index of poets   171

Introduction

Although the word 'decolonisation' emerged in the mid-twentieth century as part of the vocabulary of anti-colonial struggle, it has its genesis in a much longer and wider history of resistance that goes back to the first indigenous people who repelled the incursions and occupations of settlers from elsewhere in Africa and the Americas. In South Africa, the term has regained prominence over the last decade as a means of describing political thought and action concerned with the ongoing work of refusing and opposing practices of subjugation and control that have their roots in colonial practice. For literature and poetry, that work has been the vigorous contestation of representations imposed from elsewhere. This anthology is an attempt to answer a pertinent question: What does decolonisation look like in the world of poetry?

Answering this question inevitably means fencing with skepticism arising from commonsensical misunderstandings of what the word refers to. 'Decolonisation' is a term that has grown dense with tension over its meaning, where it might be applied and what its implications might be. It may, for some, conjure up visions of anarchic destruction, the loss of cherished values, and the dismantling of working systems. This is decolonisation as instability. For others, decolonisation begins with the admission that the structures, values or systems are fatally inadequate and in need of change. This is decolonisation in its affective sense, as it pertains to how the conditions of the present are experienced. In South Africa, wealth and poverty have been staging ever more dramatic contestations as their proximity grows closer and more unbearable.

Put simply, decolonisation is an organising tool for addressing the distance between the world as we would like it to be and as it is now. Decolonisation asks us to think about our protocols for thinking in common by questioning who has been excluded from the processes by which the stories we tell about ourselves are formed. It is thus also about whose version of the present should be allowed to obtain as a starting point for creating new worlds. The contestation that occurs at this site of dispute makes for unstable ground, where what is being fought over creates intensities of feeling that do not need to wait for defining or clarifying before they are expressed.

The past three decades have borne witness to a ratcheting-up of structural violence into direct action that is chaotic, messy and unable to be contained in pre-existing epistemic silos. The Marikana massacre, in which 34 miners at the Lonmin platinum mine near Rustenburg in the North West Province were shot dead by policemen, was an event of spectacular exemplarity. But it was also readily available for reading in terms of previous scenes of violence: Marikana, with its stark images of perforated dying and dead Black bodies, has drawn comparisons to the Sharpeville massacre of 1960, and the state-sponsored violence of the Bisho massacre in 1992. Similarly, the spectacular eruption of disorder on university campuses, heralded spectacularly by the arrival of the #RhodesMustFall movement and subsequent demands for the decolonisation of learning institutions, bears comparison to the 1976 Soweto student uprisings against Bantu education and the implementation of Afrikaans-language instruction. Thinking through events like Marikana and Rhodes Must Fall as being enfolded in a historical moment that is simultaneously experienced both as present and past, testifies to how this structural violence is sustained enough to become a perverse kind of ordinariness.

Thus, it should pass as unremarkable that out-of-scale disagreements have become part of the ordinary fabric of South African political life. As cultural theorist Hedley Twidle remarks:

> The twenty years since the advent of democracy have seen the onset of an uncompromising, expressionist, non-negotiable politics from a new generation no longer willing to wait for 'transformation', and speaking instead in terms of a total breach with the modalities of 'negotiated settlement'. In its place come a cultural tactics of anger, impatience, disruption, refusal and shutdown – whether of parliament, the State of the Nation address, the national highway or the university – in order to arrest the status quo of the present. [1]

Under conditions where structural disorder has so saturated the scene that its occurrence has become commonplace, tracing the circuits and flows of disaffection, disappointment and other often incoherent modes of public feeling helps us to make sense of the reeling present. In this regard, I want to propose that poetry is a useful lens through which to view the present scene of anxiety. Poetry is a form of art that appears in the world when someone decides to pose questions. Poetry enlists an addressee, who may be a listener or a reader, by asking us to pause before an assemblage of words or a linguistic structure. Each user brings their own forms of sense-making to the event of the poem, and it is in the creative interplay between words as they are arranged by the poet and subjectivity as it is created by the listener or receiver, that meaning arrives.

If we talk of decolonial poetry, are we saying that poetry is in need of decolonisation? Yes, in many ways that is exactly what is being said. Poetry is not inherently liberatory. Like all art, poetry is a technology of the imagination, and its workings involve those aspects of our humanity – feeling, mortality, intuition – that are enigmatic, that cannot easily be intuited. But that technology is programmed by narratives, mythologies, and ideologies that outline value in particular ways. Thus, poetry is not neutral: it is in fact deeply structured by the same biases and beliefs that undergird structural inequalities. What poetry is considered to be mainstream, what is encouraged or avoided, and what is 'included' or 'tolerated' in studies, collections and syllabi, are deeply structured decisions whose contestation forms part of the work of decolonisation. As readers, it behooves us to pay attention to who poetry is created for, who is excluded, and what falls outside the dominant processes of value production. This is where the poetry of decolonisation does its work: In these new scenes of thought, we glimpse the lives of others and we learn.

In making this argument, I would also suggest that poetry has historically functioned as a medium for thinking and recording resistance to colonialism by, in Pumla Gqola's words, 'placing the creative and the explicitly critical alongside one another'.[2] The poems gathered here are a historical archive of decolonial thinking, presented in the voice and idiom of Africans resisting their displacement from the world. Reading these poems, we move between the political and private in ways that provide us with the means to answer questions about our present. Thinking with poetry in this way brings us to the realisation that terms like 'protest poetry', 'Black Consciousness Poetry', 'Soweto Poetry', 'Township poetry' are really contingent placeholders for talking about the work that poetry does. What is made over-visceral in the South African context by these tags, might be quite readily perceived as generic affordances that reveal less than they purport to. The point of departure here, then, is to break these poems out of their generic categories. In the early poetry of Nontsizi Mgqwetho, BW Vilakazi, SEK Mqayi and others, we see an awareness that, as HIE Dhlomo put it, 'The African people's cultural struggle is as important as the political because both aim at establishing the African as a free citizen.' What these genres of poetry do, beyond recording struggle and abjection, is capture feelings in the clasp of a destabilised historical present, the better to make alternative structures of agency and affect imaginable.

With this work in mind, I want to suggest a way of understanding 'decolonisation' in relation to poetry, in a way that does not approach it as a noun describing events that have happened and can thus be readily summarised. Decolonisation is not a completed thing that can be codified as a genre (a genre is a mode of collective recognition). It is an always-in-progress mode of knowledge-creation as well as a radical knowledge movement that is used here to index a way of communicating thoughts about the historical present. But the term also gestures to the unusual temporality of combining poems that occupy multiple historical realities. What links Oswald Mtshali's caustic reflections in 'Always A Suspect' with Khadija Heeger's 'Citizen Minus'? They speak to realities that require an improvised set of responses, that is to say, responses that arise organically or without the certainty that any actions will bring about resolution.

This collection does not attempt to displace more comprehensive sweeps of the South African poetic field. One might take a leaf from Michael Chapman's *The New Century of South African Poetry*, perhaps the most comprehensive reference work and guide to the field of South African poetry, in reading the poems gathered here as conveying a necessarily 'uneven' sense of a literary culture that is constantly and restlessly remaking itself.[3] Accordingly, this volume does not present a survey of everything that might be termed the poetry of decolonisation. To provide anything like a ground plan of poetry that fits into this category would produce a meaninglessly vast tome. Instead, I have brought together different poems, spread chronologically from the mid-twentieth century to the second decade of the twenty-first century. The earlier poems represent the historical utterances of poets who took stock of their situation and loosed words in rebellion and contestation. The newer poems represent a deliberately uneven spread of work by poets writing in the wake of the earlier poets, to a present that began some time ago, and evidently means to carry on in its current mood of uncertainty. By putting them together here, I mean to suggest that there might be something fruitful in tracking thematic or conceptual repetitions across time. What similarities occur in how poets experience their different intensities of dissatisfaction? What divergences can be noticed?

Historically, the work of decolonisation in South African poetry has been in the form of a mode of thought whose central metaphors arrange themselves around the problematising of existing forms of power. The poets who were writing in the 60s, 70s and 80s were grappling with the vexed issue of how to define new racial identities. A generation of disenfranchised young South Africans sought new ways of making sense of the political conditions of life they found themselves exposed to. Those conditions were offensive and desperate enough to create a gnawing lack that could only be expressed via radical resistance. Poetry emerged as one instantiation of the felt desire for a stimulating and nourishing mode of representation profoundly suitable to speaking about the lives of the multitudes who suffered, who were deprived or injured under apartheid.

During this time, some of the most ambitious writing to emerge from South Africa was in the form of protest poetry.

Figures like Mongane Serote, Ingoapele Madingoane, Sipho Sepamla, Oswald Mtshali, Chris van Wyk, and many others, created poetry that is experimental, attuned, incisive, critical, introspective and outward-reaching. The tone of their poems is rancorous, bemused, frustrated, grieving or enraged. But each in their way is a testament to the struggle to understand the world their writers occupied.

This collection brings this older poetry into conversation with newer poetry from after 1994. In doing so, I want to suggest that there might be something fruitful in reading the anticolonial poetry of the mid-twentieth century which worked against the restrictions of apartheid alongside the poetry of the postcolony that takes aim at the bittersweet discontents of colonialism's afterlife. This is the poetry produced by the contemporary conditions of each poet's time, lived poetry, poetry of experience. These poems, though they may speak to radically different circumstances, demonstrate a commensurate density and texture that makes them legible to each other as part of the same poetics of resistance.

To speak of such an afterlife is to acknowledge that South Africa, like many formerly colonised countries, underwent a transition where the revolutionary future seemed tantalisingly close at hand. The initial optimism of the post-1994 years was galvanized by a desire for a seemingly imminent future in which the problems of the present – lack of housing, uneven resource distribution – were magically dispensed with. The inevitable encroachment of social reality thus occasioned a wide-spread sense of dissatisfaction expressed as a confrontation between those whose precarity grows ever greater with each year, and the state that demands its citizens respect its legitimacy. The philosopher Achille Mbembe glosses this as 'a negative moment' where 'new antagonisms emerge while old ones remain unresolved'.[4] Alongside the continuities of old crises, new or newly-manifesting issues – misogynistic and

LGBTQI-targeted crime and violence, xenophobia, gentrification – are unfolding in ways that threaten survival for many of those who live in this moment.

In post-apartheid South Africa, dissatisfaction is a subject of much theorisation,[5] endless speculation and other forms dedicated to explaining the antagonisms of the historical present. The story of what happened to South Africa after 1994 has been told in any number of richly detailed and necessarily rigorous studies. From these emerges what can be (and often is) parsed in a pre-fab narrative: the end of the Mandela presidency, which coincides with growing disillusionment amid concerns of mounting crime and corruption, and the general dissolution of public certainty from the Mbeki years through to widespread opprobrium under the presidency of Jacob Zuma. The decommissioning of the Rainbow Nation mythology has coincided with a rise in anxiety for those who have structural privilege. The latter experience the present as a precarious space where things are spiralling out of control, beyond the capacity of the state to arrest the cracks and conserve what remains. As people have begun to disinvest from a Rainbow Nation fantasy that has been downscaled and decontented beyond tolerance, so the sentimental collective optimism (whose subscription was anyway dependent on what resources you had available to you) has given way to dissatisfaction as the genre through which public life is experienced.

These poems are placed here because they represent the voices of poets who are mobilised by their distance from an ideal world. Things are not right, they say; but let us imagine what it would take to make them so. The poetry of decolonisation disturbs the easy ordering of the world according to logics that make prejudice and discrimination invisible. The energy powering this disturbance is the energy of those who use their words to anticipate a new world, because they can no longer stand to live in the present one.

Thus runs the work of decolonial poetry. I am not suggesting any kind of structural uniformity to these poems. They occupy concurrent realities. There is no way to adequately fence off something that we might then call the content of decolonisation, since the term denotes a form of knowledge production, rather than a period of time. While the contents of this collection arise from the specificity of the South African milieu, their perspectives are applicable to wider literary communities. Each of these works deals with the issue of how to create a different kind of logic structure that allows for engaging with the world in another manner.

It might be more productive to talk of decolonial poetry as occurring in the moment of impasse. If the apartheid moment occasioned the need for people to respond to it in assertive ways, South Africa post-1994 has seen the rise of new problems and a growing sense of disillusionment around the rise in gender-based violence, continued structural inequality, and the perceived sense that things are going backwards rather than progressing forwards. Nevertheless, what has currently transpired in the context of South African decolonisation requires greater contextualisation. As South Africa has moved from Rainbow Nationism through ambivalence and into anxiety, Ivan Vladislavic's description of the postcolony as 'a second interregnum, a parenthetical era, in which a provisional country asserts itself, but drags its history behind it in brackets' seems more apt than ever.[6] It is clear that although the disaster known as apartheid has been formally dismantled, many of the psychic obstacles built by the vast machinery of separate development remained behind. Not only did they remain behind, but they were also joined by a constellation of new authoritarianisms, newly visible modes of social violence, and new forms of predation that conspire to reverse or throttle any collective sense of freedom. When we read these voices together, a story of South African decolonisation emerges. It is a story that offers an aesthetic history of poetic freedom-making.

This book draws together a diverse array of poems speaking to events and experiences and moments of being that overlap, converge or diverge at various points. By setting them down here, we endeavour to keep up with the insurgent energies these poems liberate through their various forms of telling the story of decolonisation. These poems enact a collective rebooting of social awareness by transforming what awareness looks like. What I want to emphasise, here, is that the poetry of decolonisation is not simply about registering dissatisfaction as the settled state of the present. It is about recognising dissatisfaction as the shared starting point for rethinking the world. Read this way, it is possible to bring together poems from many different temporalities as decolonial. JJR Jolobe's 'The Making of a Servant' is placed in a new sort of aesthetic frame that enables it to take on a new materiality alongside other poetic objects.

Certainly, the last decade has born witness to a new generation of South African poets whose contributions critically engage with the idea of a sociopolitical landscape devoid of alternatives. These poets have lived through the complex vicissitudes of a post-apartheid South Africa whose optimism has been damaged by the failure of various democracy experiments and the perceived absconding of the state from its responsibilities to the citizenry. Against the various ways in which the democratic state has disappointed, defrauded, defunded or despoiled its population, continued structural inequality and other frayings of the social compact, the work of these poets pays attention to the effects of this change. For these contemporary poets, the occasioning of a state of precarity is what ties them to the historical past; their subject matter is a virtual commons made real by the poetry of decolonisation.

The poets I have chosen here are a sampling of what constitutes a rich and diverse poetic community. There are no doubt many great poets who have not been included here, just as there will be many instructive poems from the past that might have merited inclusion, but were left off the list. Again, the aim is not to create a grand totalising picture of the poetry of decolonisation, but to suggest a few directions from which it may be witnessed. After all, much of this poetry already has a place in the South African cultural imaginary. To call them decolonial is not to invent them, but rather to bring them over to an altered order of meaning and value in which they are not simply stylistic curiosities on an otherwise-white timeline. It is to ask what it is in this poetry that allows us to think about dissolution of the old as the foundation for new possibilities.

In Mjele Msimang's incendiary poem 'born(e) to the grave', for example, we see a pained unpicking of national mythology:

i may have been born on 27 April 1994 –
but i was never born free.

as long as we pay homage to statues
of colonial laws that decided how bodies
language
their own love,
i was never born free

With such a broad diversity of poems, there must obviously be some divergences. The earlier poetry is marked by a sense of 'talking back', as well as the presence of what was usually read by critics as a compulsion towards the direct moral appeal – whereas the poetry of the post-apartheid moment addresses itself to different anxieties of living.

In much of the later poetry, we see a preoccupation with the inescapable sense that the desired emancipation has not come to pass, or indeed, that the expected freedoms of the current order have been perverted. These are poems impelled by ambivalence and doubt. Witness Khadija Heeger remarking that

> Somewhere between here and there
> between 1994 and the present
> I was lost on the periphery of a South African story.
> ('Citizen Minus')

This anthology brings together a selection of poets writing in the twentieth and twenty-first centuries, whose work is oriented around the liberation from forms of subjugation, and with the formation of a voice and a position from which to speak about their experiences. The poetry gathered here forms a whole that is not meant to stand as a definitive statement on decolonial poetry. Rather, we endeavour to illustrate the ways South African poets have challenged the boundaries placed around who can speak, whose voice is granted authority, and who has the right to author history. These poems, arranged as they are, yield a richly textured picture of the workings of decoloniality in the twentieth and twenty-first centuries. In reading them, we are invited to think about what things have been broken by colonialism, what can be repaired, and what is irreparable. Only by doing so can we begin the work of thinking about what new structures will replace the ones we live with today.

I am gesturing here towards the corrective work happening in much of this poetry. Where much attention was given to 'struggle poetry' written by men, the voices of others have been drowned out or their poetry rendered unseen. This is to say that while much of the early poetry of South Africa's protest movement assumed a collective position from which to speak, we now know that not everybody can assume their inhabitation of this collectivised subjectivity. The great proliferation of poetry produced by women after apartheid is a deliberate action against the historical tendency to locate decolonial experiences in ways that deny the kinds of knowledge, resistance and world-making produced by women. Puleng Lange Stewart's propulsive words:

And then – Yes
– young black female –
Be Aggressive
Bare your teeth!

direct us to notice womxn's voices as powerful agents of political engagement. By situating these poems in proximity to older histories of exclusion, what comes to the foreground is not simply the need to end such exclusion, but to interrupt the standpoint from which such exclusions make sense.

To be sure, the range and diversity of voices assembled here allows us to think in more and different kinds of ways about how we can make new and better worlds happen. In this regard, the collection presents poetry in a way that works without a hierarchy of values. Framed in this way, there is no scale of prestige between the poetry of Wally Serote and the newer work of less storied poets. Poets take words that are available to everybody. What matters here is use: how might we read this poetry in a way that enables us to understand decolonisation as something that happens in practice, and therefore as a process animated by situated, conflicting, contradictory and dialogic impulses? Knitting together these voices allows for new potentialities to be produced. The animating impulse behind this collection of voices old and new is to allow us to perceive how different South African poets have placed their work in the world, and how that work might relate to the struggle for radical social transformation, and how it might be put right. This collection is thus a space for story to flourish: for correctives and re-memberings and in-fills of absence. It is a space for talking back, for unsilencing quieted voices, for interrupting and for fleshing out local meanings. It is the site of decolonisation in practice.

Wamuwi Mbao
Stellenbosch

---

1 Twidle, Hedley. *Experiments with Truth: Narrative Non-fiction and the Coming of Democracy in South Africa*. James Currey, 2019. p 186–187.
2 Gqola, Pumla. 'Whirling worlds? Women's poetry, feminist imagination and contemporary South African publics'. *Scrutiny2* 16(2), 2011, p 5.
3 Chapman, Michael. *The New Century of South African Poetry*. 3rd ed. Johannesburg: Ad Donker Publishers, 2018.
4 Mbembe, Achille. Decolonizing Knowledge and the Question of the Archive. Lecture delivered at the Wits Institute for Social and Economic Research. Retrieved from wiser.wits.ac.za. Accessed 25 January 2020.
5 See Hedley Twidle's *Experiments with Truth*, Pumla Gqola's *What is Slavery to Me? Postcolonial/Slave Memory in Post-apartheid South Africa* (Wits University Press, 2010), Leon de Kock's *Losing the Plot: Reality and Fiction in Postapartheid Writing* (Wits University Press, 2016), Eusebius McKaiser's essay collections *A Bantu in my Bathroom! Debating Race, Sexuality and other uncomfortable South African topics* (Pan Macmillan, 2012) and *Run Racist Run: Journeys into the Heart of Racism* (Pan Macmillan, 2016), amongst others.
6 Vladislavic, Ivan. *Willem Boshoff*. Houghton: David Krut Publishing, 2005. p 88.

Pre-Sharpeville (1890–1960)

Africa: My Native Land
Mrs AC Dube

How beautiful are thy hills and thy dales!
I love thy very atmosphere so sweet,
Thy trees adorn the landscape rough and steep
No other country in the whole world could with thee compare.

It is here where our noble ancestors
Experienced joys of dear ones and of homes;
Where great and glorious kingdoms rose and fell,
Where blood was shed to save thee, thou dearest land ever known.

But, alas! Their efforts were all in vain
For today others claim thee as their own
No longer can their offspring cherish thee,
No land to call their own – but outcasts in their own country.

Despair of thee I never, never will,
Struggle I must for freedom – God's great gift –
Till every drop of blood within my veins
Shall dry upon my troubled bones, oh thou Dearest Native Land.

'Civilised' Labour Policy
lr

Hertzog is my shepherd; I am in want.
He maketh me to lie down on park benches.
He leadeth me beside still factories.
He arouseth my doubt of his intention.
He leadeth me in the path of destruction for his Party's sake.
Yea, I walk through the valley of the shadow of destruction
And I fear evil, for thou art with me,
The Politicians and the Profiteers, they frighten me,
Thou preparest a reduction in my salary before me,
In the presence of mine enemies.
Thou anointest mine income with taxes,
My expense runneth over.
Surely unemployment and poverty will follow me
All the days of this Administration
And I shall dwell in a mortgaged house forever.

The Making of a Servant
Translated from the Xhosa
JJR Jolobe

I can no longer ask how it feels
To be choked by a yoke-rope
Because I have seen it for myself in the chained ox.
The blindness has left my eyes. I have become aware,
I have seen the making of a servant
In the young yoke-ox.

He was sleek, lovely, born for freedom,
Not asking anything from anyone, simply
    priding himself on being a young ox.
Someone said: Let him be caught and
    trained and broken in,
Going about it as if he meant to help him.
I have seen the making of a servant
In the young yoke-ox.

He tried to resist, fighting for his freedom.
He was surrounded, fenced in with wisdom and experience.
They overcame him by trickery: 'He must be trained.'
A good piece of rationalisation can camouflage evil.
I have seen the making of a servant
In the young yoke-ox.

He was bound with ropes that cut into his head,
He was bullied, kicked, now and again petted,
But their aim was the same: to put a yoke on him.
Being trained in one's own interests is for the privileged.

I have seen the making of a servant
In the young yoke-ox.

The last stage. The yoke is set on him.
They tie the halter round his neck, slightly choking him.
They say the job's done, he'll be put to work with
    the others
To obey the will of his power and taskmaster.
I have seen the making of a servant
In the young yoke-ox.

He kicks out, trying to break away.
They speak with their whips. He turns backwards
Doing his best to resist but then they say: 'Hit him.'
A prisoner is a coward's plaything.
I have seen the making of a servant
In the young yoke-ox.

Though he stumbled and fell, he was bitten on the tail.
Sometimes I saw him raking at his yoke-mate
With his horns – his friend of a minute, his blood-brother.
The suffering under the yoke makes for bad blood.
I have seen the making of a servant
In the young yoke-ox.

The sky seemed black as soft rain fell.
I looked at his hump, it was red,
Dripping blood, the mark of resistance.
He yearns for his home, where he was free.
I have seen the making of a servant
In the young yoke-ox.

Stockstill, tired, there was no sympathy.
He bellowed notes of bitterness.
They loosened his halter a little – to let him breathe,
They tightened it again, snatching back his breath.
I have seen the making of a servant
In the young yoke-ox.

I saw him later, broken, trained.
Pulling a double-shared plough through deep soil,
Serving, struggling for breath, in pain.
To be driven is death. Life is doing things for yourself.
I have seen the making of a servant
In the young yoke-ox.

I saw him climb the steepest of roads.
He carried heavy loads, staggering –
The mud of sweat which wins profit for another.
The savour of working is a share in the harvest.
I have seen the making of a servant
In the young yoke-ox.

I saw him hungry with toil and sweat,
Eyes all tears, spirit crushed.
No longer able to resist. He was tame.
Hope lies in action aimed at freedom.
I have seen the making of a servant
In the young yoke-ox.

The Gold Mines
Translated from the Zulu
BW Vilakazi

Roar and clang, you machines of the mines,
Roar from dawn till darkness falls;
I shall wake, O let me be!
Roar, machines, continue deaf
To black men groaning as they labour
Tortured by their aching muscles,
Gasping in the fetid air,
Reeking from the dirt and sweat,
Shaking their bodies desperately.

Bellow you frenzied bulls of steel!
Far is that place where first you came to life
And – roasted by fiery furnaces
Until you were ready and only ash remained –
Were quickly dispatched, and having crossed the sea
Were loaded on trucks, for puffing fuming engines
To bring you to Goli, place of gold, and us.
Loudly you bellowed, till we, like frightened dassies
Swarming towards you, answered your strident summons.

These dassies, each and all, were black,
And, shorn of their tails, you captured them;
Then you pushed them down the mine,
Exploited them and drained their strength.
Turn you tireless wheels of steel!
I know you did not choose to come
And cause us all this drudgery.
For you no less enslaved, must toil and roar

Till, one by one, worn out you rot
On some neglected rubbish plot.

Sometimes, as I walk along the road,
I turn to look at you and wonder
If you as well beget each other,
Increase and multiply! – How vain a thought!
Yet we are brothers, for we like you, must rot,
Be shattered and exploited in the mines
Until, with damaged lungs and ebbing strength
We cough without relief, collapse and die.
But you are spared that fatal coughing – Why?

Around the noisy compounds of the mines,
We hear that black men born of many tribes
Had come to raise these great white dumps,
Astounding to their ancestors.
Yes, when a siren screeched one day
A poor black dassie heard its call
And answering its summons, in confusion
Was trapped, and then, transformed into a mole,
Was forced to burrow deep and search for gold.

Soon swarms of puzzled dassies came to join it:
Then swiftly rose the great white dumps:
Deep were the holes and high the hills –
Sandlwana itself is now no higher!
Sweating I climb them, reach the top
And watch the dust like clouds of smoke
I see them swirling there beneath me
Forever obscuring the sullied earth.

Roar and clang, you machines of the mines!
Thunder loudly and louder yet.
Drown our voices with your clamour,
Stifle our cries and groans of pain
The while you eat away our joints.
Mock us, old tyrants, callous and mighty.
Let our suffering cause your laughter!
Too well we know your terrible powers,
For you are the masters – we the slaves!

When we agreed to leave our huts
Be herded like oxen, forget we are men,
We left our mealies and creamy milk
To eat this lumpy, soggy porridge.
Our manhood diminished and known as 'boys'
We all must acknowledge our world has changed;
Now, wakened at dawn, we stand in lines,
Thinking – how strange to be interred,
Open-eyed creatures buried alive!

Roar, as you will, machines of the mines!
I am awake and never dawdle;
See I am going underground
To shatter the rock-face with my pick;
And you above, though hearing nothing,
Will know I wield the white man's drill
Because you see the little trolleys
Filled with stones of white and green.

My brother also carries a pick
Heaves a spade upon his shoulder,
Drags on his feet a miner's boots

And enters the shaft to follow me.
The earth soon swallows us who burrow,
And, if I perish underground,
What does it matter, who am I?
Day after day, O, fellow men! –
I, helpless, watch my brother collapse.

Where I have come from, far away,
The lands are free of towering buildings
Whose tops I stretch my neck to see;
But when I return there, clutching my bundle,
All I can find are shrivelled stalks
And empty huts; I scratch my head
And ask about my family.
They answer: 'Ask your white employer!' –
I close my mouth in weary silence.

Roar, still louder, machines of the mines!
Though far away in Germiston.
Your clamour penetrates my soul
And echoes in my ears
Like distant bells of booming brass;
They bring to mind the giant buildings
Owned by men enriched by me
Who daily exploit my sweated toil,
While I, the proverbial church mouse, starve.

Yet, thunder more softly, you harsh machines!
Because the white man's heart is stone,
Must you be pitiless too, O steel?
Silence your uproar in the mines
And listen I beg you to all our pleas,

Or else we too may have no pity
When, on that day the future hides,
We cry at last: 'O things of iron,
You are the slaves of black men now!'

Beware! Though now my hands are empty,
These puny arms, in days gone by,
Wielded the fatal assagais,
Which as we hurled them, darkened the earth.
Great Queen Victoria's realm was shaken,
Paul Kruger's soldiers terrified –
And yet we were defeated!
But still I dream – O steel contraptions! –
That lands our fathers once possessed
Shall, by their sons be ruled again.

Today I have no place to rest
Beneath dark clouds of alien power;
Our fathers' fields lie barren now,
Untilled by men all cowed like me.
For even if I owned great wealth,
This land my father's fathers owned,
I never may purchase or possess.
O, mighty spirits of heaven and earth! –
Will you not end this vile oppression?

Down in our fathers' resting place
Where you, our ancestral spirits dwell,
They say your powers are unsurpassed
When you commune with God
Who sees the man – but not his colour! –
Here, earth is reddened with my blood

That clots and dries in savage heat
While I, exhausted, pray to you –
But hear no echo in reply.

O see how day by day this land
Is being plundered by those who seized it –
These foreigners who enrich themselves
While I and my deprived black brothers
Are landless, penniless, empty-handed!
Above the mine-pits grass is green,
Vivid as heaven's blest horizon,
Where dwell the spirits to whom we pray –
But they, alas, are silent still!

How loud your roar, machines of the mines!
My hands are torn,
My feet are swollen,
They throb, but where are remedies? –
White men's medicines cost much money!
Hush, you machines, and spare my ears!
Well have I served my rich white masters, –
Bot O my soul is heavy within me!

Subdue your thunder! I long to sleep,
Close tight my eyes, hear nothing more,
And dread no longer tomorrow's dawn.
I yearn to sleep and wake afar
Where I may know among the spirits,
Repose unmarred by earthly turmoil,
When I, enwrapped by ancestral arms,
Shall rest at last in heaven's own green pastures.

Freedom's Child
Peter Abrahams

The echoes are dying,
The whisper is gone,
But every tree seems to nod its head,
Is it its ghost …?

I

I am China
They call me Le-Yen,
The ricefields own me.
My best years are gone;
I have sweated,
Eaten opium,
And at last I died –
And now I'm going to die again.
But I've heard it, this whisper,
And I love its sound.
I'm China,
But they call me Le-Yen down here.

II

And I am a mother,
Some call me Japan.
I don't want an Empire,
Or a wonderful navy,
I don't care what rate I am –
I have no fight –
All I want

Is my son to return
And food for the children,
A dress for my daughter,
My afternoon tea.
And no uniforms.
I want peace, I want quiet
And my children's love.
That whisper –
What promise does it hold …?

III

My name is Coolie. Untouchable.
I am a jewel,
The brightest in a crown
Of a foreign king.
From my blood
Princes make gold to weight themselves.
I'm an Anna a day, I spit blood when I cough.
I am the floods
And a hundred million starving souls.
I am the droughts
And a hundred million dead.
I am Nehru
I languish in jail.
I am an Anand –
The tears of a tortured soul.
But I've heard this whisper,
My body grows
Bigger!
BIGGER!!
Now there's room for me only here –

No kings or princes.
And I cry:
'Inquilab Zindabad!'
I am India!

IV

I am the gold mines,
Paying huge dividends;
I am the preacher –
Shining car, well fed;
My sermon is race purity,
And God was white and
White men must guard blacks.
I am the banker, Kipling,
And East and West
And the white man's burden.
I am the Institute of Race Relations,
And racial mixture is a crime …
I am a half-caste –
Racial mixture is a crime …
I am gold,
Fashioned out of beads of sweat of black men;
I am segregation and the pass-law;
I'm eight million slaves …
But somewhere, too,
I nurture a volcano,
And out of love
I shall cause a wild eruption
With an aftermath of laughter

V

Slaves of masters, world without choice,
Serving those masters I still bear your voice;
The great lords who rule you are heading for death,
They suck in its vapour with every breath.
Bending your backs to tyranny's yoke,
Taking the full force of every stroke,
The master beasts are marching to death –
I heard it whispered in a dying breath.
The whisper was caught by the Proletarian breeze
And carried away across the seas,
And every sufferer heard the voice,
And in quiet I heard the wind rejoice.
And clear in the twilight the clouds burst wild,
Singing my song – 'Freedom's Child!'

Because I'm Black
HIE Dhlomo

Because I'm black
You think I lack
The talents, feelings and ambitions
That others have;
You do not think I crave positions
That others crave.

Because the people eat and sing
And mate,
You do not see their suffering.
You rate
Them fools
And tools
Of those with power and boastful show;
Not Fate, but fault, has made things so.

Beware! these people, struggling, hold
The last trump card;
Subdue them now you may
'Tis but delay. Another day
When God commands they will be bold …
They will strike hard!

Post-Sharpeville (1960–1976)

Always a Suspect
Mbuyiseni Oswald Mtshali

I get up in the morning
and dress up like a gentleman –
A white shirt a tie and a suit.

I walk into the street
to be met by a man
who tells me 'to produce'.

I show him
the document of my existence
to be scrutinized and given the nod.

Then I enter the foyer of a building
to have my way barred by a commissionaire
'What do you want?'

I trudge the city pavements
side by side with 'madam'
who shifts her handbag
from my side to the other,
and looks at me with eyes that say
'Ha! Ha! I know who you are;
beneath those fine clothes
ticks the heart of a thief.'

The Pension Jiveass
Mandlenkosi Langa

I lead her in,
A sepia figure 100 years old.
Blue ice chips gaze
And a red slash gapes:
'What does she want?'
I translate: 'Pension, sir.'
'Useless kaffir crone,
Lazy as the black devil.
She'll get fuck-all.'
I translate.
'My man toiled
And rendered himself impotent
With hard labour.
He paid tax like you.
I am old enough to get pension.
I was born before the great wars
And saw my father slit your likes' throats!'
I don't translate, but
She loses her pension anyhow.

The Miners
Mafika Mbuli

This dungeon
Makes the mind weary
Kneaded with the sight of
A million stones
Passing through my hands
I see the flesh sticking like hair
On thorns
Against the grating rocks
Of these hills dug for gold,
And life is bitter here.
Crawling through the day
In a sleepwalker's dream,
Frightening the night away with my snores,
I dream of the diminished breath
Of miners planted in the stones –
The world is not as ease
But quakes under the march of our boots
Tramping the dust under our feet …
Click, clack, our picks knock for life
Until the eyes are dazed
Counting the rubble of scattered stones.

Day and night are one.
But I know each day dawns
And the heated sun licks every shrub dry
While we who burrow the earth
Tame the dust with our lungs.

Click, clack, we knock with picks
And our minds
Drone with the voices of women
Harassing our loins
To force courage into the heart.
Wherefore might we scorn their sacrifice
Made in blood,
Greater that the blood of men
Sacrificed to the earth
For its possession!
And so
Clap, scrape
With our hands manacled
With weariness
We mine
All our lives
Till the mind is numb
And ceases to ask …

Kneel and Pray
Nkathazo ka Mnyayiza

I have seen many white stars,
but haven't seen any black;
        but i know that
one day

        from the north
the long black star will come;
black clouds then will scud around it,

    then

        when it shakes

you'll shiver like reeds,

    then
        when it screams

you'll kneel and pray.

The Man of Smoke
Njabulo S Ndebele

Strapped to my aunt's back
I find warmth
We walk through many streets
I don't know which,
but I know when we turn.
Even in my blanket,
I can feel the dust of the wind
pecking at me, like many needles,
but I cling to my aunt,
her back is warm and moist.

There are voices in this house
I don't know which,
I'm in the warm darkness
of my blanket.
'Mzalwane' Voices greet,
'Bazalwane' auntie answers.
Then I am unstrapped
to the gaze of silence
to the gloom of a candle
to the frightening stares
of a huge face of a person of wood
with teeth as big as fingers
smoke comes out of his mouth,
smoke comes out of his wicked smile.

Put me back, auntie, put me back,
it is cold here
but my words are not lips

they are my hands
clutching at her dress.

She puts me under a table,
but I move out to a corner.
A drum begins the beat:
GOGOM GOM ..... GOGOM GOM .....
and there is song and dance
wild song and dance
and I am watching alone
from a corner; my corner.
I am wide eyed
I am shorter than the table
and dancing legs are massive pillars.
I cling to my corner
lest I am crushed by dance.
I cling to my corner
watching my aunt do funny things;
she is mad, quite mad:
all are mad here,
and smoke issues out of
the ugly person's mouth,
smoke is filling the room,
the room is grey smoke now,
GOGOM GOM ..... GOGOM GOM .....
Alleluya! Alleluya ....
round round round they dance
round the table
GOGOM GOM .....GOGOM GOM .....
Alleluya! Alleluya .....

I am a child watching
from a corner
I am a child clinging
to my corner

I am a child fearing
to be crushed.
I watch my aunt who is mad
quite mad.
All are mad here.
They kneel before the face of smoke
they cry, they shriek,
they breathe in gasps
they say a wind must enter them
they are mad quite mad,
rising to sing and dance and clap hands.
I fear.
I fear people with the wind, praying
like a cow bellowing.

Strapped to my aunt's back,
I find warmth
we walk through many streets
I don't know which,
but I know we are going home now.
I know that we are passing other people
singing, drumming and hand-clapping
down the street:
'These are the wicked dogs
who broke away from our sect
'Curse them, God. May they burn.'
Even in the noise of the wind

I can hear auntie's spittle
cursing the dogs on the tarred road.

But I am warm in the blanket,
it is dark and warm and moist inside,
and I dream of the man of wood
standing next to my bed in the dark,
choking me with his smoke,
and I cry.
'Poor boy, you are hungry,' auntie says.

Location Fires
Jennifer Davids

Beneath my eyelids
the landscape is heavy
the people are buried in ground-
clinging shapes of houses

From Langa to Nyanga
the fires are hidden
the landscape is flattened
frightened and silenced

Where are the fires
for me to believe in
where are the tongues of flame
to lick and conquer the dark

In answer the black body
of the sky rears up
loud with roaring
voices of the stars

The stars tonight
are blue backyard fires
studding the black
location of the sky

What's in this Black 'Shit'
Mongane Wally Serote

It is not the steaming little rot
In the toilet bucket,
It is the upheaval of the bowels
Bleeding and coming out through the mouth
And swallowed back,
Rolling in the mouth,
Feeling its taste and wondering what's next like it.

Now I'm talking about this;
'Shit' you hear an old woman say,
Right there, squeezed in her little match-box
With her fatness and gigantic life experience,
Which makes her a child,
'Cause the next day she's right there,
Right there serving tea to the woman
Who's lying in bed at 10 a.m. sick with wealth,
Which she's prepared to give her life for
'Rather than you marry my son or daughter.'

This 'Shit' can take the form of action;
My younger sister under the full weight of my father,
And her face colliding with his steel hand,
''Cause she spilled sugar that I work so hard for'
He says, not feeling satisfied with the damage his hands
Do to my yelling little sister.

I'm learning to pronounce this 'Shit' well,
Since the other day,
At the pass office,

When I went to get employment,
The officer there endorsed me to Middelburg,
So I said, hard and with all my might, 'Shit!'
I felt a little better;
But what's good, is, I said it in his face,
A thing my father wouldn't dare do.
That's what's in this black 'Shit'.

Getting off the Ride
Mafika Gwala

I

I get off the bus ride
after long standing
listening to black voices
that obliviate the traffic noises;
A billboard overwhelms me,
Like an ugly plastic monster with fiercy eyes
it tells me what canned drink
will be good enough to quench my thirst;
I eye-mock the plastic arrogance
'Cos I know, shit, I know
I'm being taken for a ride.

II

Past this Patel's shop
The hustling efforts of these youngsters
almost urge me into seriously viewing
their imitation wrist watches,
When I know they are wanting to drain me
of the few Rands I'm still left with –
So's their brothers can get to the top drop;
And me to go on entering shops
– throwing my last Rands each time;
Ya, I know I'm being taken for a ride.

III

At the cinema house
the big poster poses a bigcrowd drawer,
I slide into the darkness;
The still blackness
is nothing but inverted blackness
cast upon imposed darkness;
I throw my eyes on the screen …
… then the long watch.
I walk out worse off,
Worse than when I mooched in;
Movies can be made to fast sell the mind
(an old warning in the family quips) like
the inflation coin at the tourist bazaar.
Again I know I've been taken for a ride.

IV

My boots jar me
as I take the corner off Grey Street
Into Victoria's busy, buzzy Victoria
Beesy Victoria's market area.
Some black mamas kneeling
their hands on the sidewalk
their second-hand clothes before them,
They kneel as if in prayer.
A white hippie bums towards them
with what shapes into a pair of
fawn corduroy jeans:
'They are fishbottomed', the aunt tilts
the deal. The seller hooks a feigned smile

with his cagey chin,
Looks like both have no choice
So the limp deal is sealed.
With unease the hippie moves off
You'd swear he's left a bomb to detonate;
I radar his moves
whilst yarning my eyes onto the mama,
the mama still on that solemn kneel
that's accompanied by sombre looks
from close range.
Where's that hippish fixer?
Into the market lanes for a blow-up;
And the black mama to scrounge a sale
after a wash of these sweaty pants
that can only be bought by some black brother
whose boss won't give him enough to afford
a pair of decent trousers.
And again I know I'm being taken for a ride.

V

I know this ride bloody well.
I'm from those squatted mothers
Those squatted mothers in the draughty air;
Those mothers selling handouts,
Those mothers selling fruits,
Those mothers selling vegetables,
Those mothers selling till dusk
in the dusty streets of Clermont, Thembisa,
Alex, Galeshewe, Dimbaza, Pietersburg.
Those mothers in dusty and tearful streets
that are found in Stanger, Mandeni, Empangeni

Hammarsdale, Mabopane, Machibisa, Soweto.
I'm one of the sons of those black mamas,
Was brought up in those dust streets;
I'm the black mama's son who vomits
on the doorstep of his shack home, pissed with
concoction. Because his world and the world
in town are as separate as the mountain ranges
and the deep sea.
I'm the naked boy
running down a muddy road,
the rain pouring bleatingly
in Verulam's Mission Station;
With the removal trucks brawling for starts
Starts leading to some stifling redbricked
ghetto of four-roomed houses at Ntuzuma.
I'm the pipeskyf pulling cat
standing in the passage behind Ndlovu's barbershop
Making dreams and dreams
Dreaming makes and makes;
Dreaming, making and making, dreaming
with poetry and drama scripts
rotting under mats
or being eaten by the rats.
I'm the staggering cat on Saturday morning's
West Street. The cat whose shattered hopes
were bottled up in beers, cane, vodka;
Hopes shattered by a system that once offered
liquor to 'Exempted Natives' only.
I'm the bitter son leaning against the lamp post
Not wishing to go to school
where his elder brother spent years, wasted years
at school wanting to be white; only to end as

messenger boy.
I'm the skollie who's thrown himself
out of a fast moving train
Just to avoid blows, kicks and the hole.
I'm one of the surviving children of Sharpeville
Whose black mothers spelled it out in blood.
I'm the skhotheni who confronts devil-eyed cops
down Durban's Grey Street …
Since he's got no way to go out.
I'm the young tsotsi found murdered in a donga
in the unlit streets of Edendale, Mdantsane.

VI

I'm the puzzled student
burning to make head and tail of Aristotle
because he hasn't heard of the buried
Kingdom of Benin or the Zimbabwe Empire,
The student who is swotting himself to madness
striving for universal truths made untrue.
I'm the black South African exile who has come
across a coughing drunk nursing his tuberculosis
on a New York pavement and remembered
he's not free.
I'm the black newspaper vendor
standing on the street corner 2 o'clock
in the morning of Sunday,
Distributing news to those night life crazy
nice-timers who will one day come into knocks
with the real news.
I'm the youthful Black with hopes of life
standing on file queue for a job

at the local chief's kraal,
This chief who has let himself and his people
into some confused Bantustan kaak
Where there's bare soil, rocks and cracking cakes
of rondavel mudbricks.
I'm the lonely poet
who trudges the township's ghetto passages
pursuing the light,
The light that can only come through a totality
of change:
Change in minds, change
Change in social standings, change
Change in means of living, change
Change in dreams and hopes, change
> Dreams and hopes that are Black
> Dreams and hopes where games end
> Dreams where there's end to man's
creation of gas chambers and concentration camps.
I'm the Africa Kwela instrumentalist whose notes
profess change.

VII

They say the Black Ghost is weak
That it is feeble
and cannot go the distance
I say that's their wishful thinking:
The Black Ghost outmanoeuvres the wiles of Raleigh
on treacherous seas,
The ghost that steamed South Pacific trains
to Florida after Tres Castillos was not black;
Which ghost spurned the wiles of Rhodes,

Rhodes treating Black hospitality as scraps
of paper?
No, I know the Black Ghost.
It has led to many victories
In the pitch darkness of dispossession;
I can sit back and watch the screen
of Black Thoughts
In which Black success is focused.
I may not have seen Spartacus, Attila
or the Maccabee brothers for that score;
I also did not see Shaka, the Kofikarikari
or Mshweshwe, Bhambatha, for another score;
And down to those Black youths with guns
in the streets of Watts, Harlem, Oakland.
The people of Guinea-Bissau shed their tears
for Cabral with the muzzles of their guns.
Sharpeville's Black Ghost haunts all racists,
Urges the Black people forward.
I live with this Ghost.
I've come to love this Ghost.
I live with the Black Ghost
When I'm dumped in soulless structures
From Windhoek to Pretoria to Pietersburg
From Gugulethu to Makhutha to Ngwelezana;
Where I'm denied understanding
according to statutes of ethnic rule;
My brothers who are caged in prisons
My brothers waiting in the dark street corners
My brothers sent to mental asylums
My brothers forced into exile
My brothers who bullshit me for a Rand
My brothers who dream of a Ford Mustang
    when they've gone to bed on empty stomachs

My brothers who'll sell their fellow brothers
    when they've lost the key to survival
My brothers who'll roll their fathers on
    Friday night.
Yes, I'm made to feel motherless, fatherless, shitless
Me with enough shit in my guts to blackshit
    any officiated shit,
Me wishing for a gun
When I know some pig will wish to collar me
for the 3-Star knife I've bought at the shop
down the street.

VIII

I hate this ride.
When I know Dudu Pukwana's horn
is blowing winter out of London's black crowds;
I hate this ride.
When I dance to Miriam Makeba
Miriam Makeba's 'Jol'iinkomo' that brings back
the proud and angry past of my ancestors
by whom tribe did not be taken for nation;
I hate this ride.
When I learn no Latin from faked classics
When 2 x 2 economics shows me it's part of the
    trick – teaching me how to starve
When Coca Cola, Pepsi Cola ads, all the sweet things
    are giving me wind in the belly;
I ask again, what is Black?
Black is when you get off the ride.
Black is point of self realization
Black is point of new reason

Black is point of: NO NATIONAL DECEPTION!
Black is point of determined stand
Black is point of TO BE or NOT TO BE for blacks
Black is point of RIGHT ON!
Black is energetic release from the shackles of Kaffir, Bantu,
    non-white.
Sometimes there's a fall
when brother gets off the ride,
And the fall hurts;
A fall is a hurt to every black brother.
Then I smell the jungle
I get the natural smell of the untamed jungle;
I'm with the mamba
I learn to understand the mamba
I become a khunga-khunga man
I'm with the Black Ghost of the skom jungle
I get the smell of phuthu in a ghetto kitchen
The ghetto, a jungle I'm learning to know
I hear the sound of African drums beating
to freedom songs;
And the sound of the Voice come:
   Khunga, Khunga!
  Untshu, Untshu!
   Funtu, Funtu!
  Shundu, Shundu!!
   Sinki, Sinki!
     Mojo, Mojo!
O-m! O--o--m! O----hhhhhhhhhhmmmm!!!
The voice speaks:
'I'm the Voice that moves with the Black Thunder
I'm the Wrath of the Moment
I strike swift and sure

I shout in the West and come from the East
I fight running battles with enemy gods
    in the black clouds
I'm the watersnake amongst watersnakes
    and fish amongst fish
I throw missiles that outspace the SAM
I leave in stealth
    and return in Black anger.
O---m! Ohhh---mmmm! O----hhhhhhmmmmmmmm!!!'

Post-Soweto (1976–)

the morning caught me
Shabbir Banoobhai

the morning caught me
reaching
for the sky

in shafts of light
i said
i'd travel home

in fire
cleanse
my song

chastened
i'd etch my want
deep in the heart of god

oh what lack of love
has caught me
lingering here

in a land where night
must come
to wash me black again

thinking about a white christmas
Fhazel Johennesse

overseas they have white christmas
snow burying everything in sight
and making it all seem soft and lovely
while down here in the south
christmas is celebrated in driving heat
i try to connect snow and christmas
i fail and then i laugh
because as i think about it
i realise that christmas down here
is really a very white affair

The Dying Ground
Monnapule Lebakeng*

(It is known that elephants, when sensing that death is near,
walk for thousands of miles to a special 'dying ground'
where they lay themselves down without food or drink until they
die ...)

The elephants came
and brought with them
a crookery of God
and brotherhood,
took our verdant land
with gunpowder and psalms
and proclaimed a covenant
in his name.

Today, the fetters bite deeper
cruelty is resolute,
genocide defined.

Beyond Azania,
black children eat manhood
from bloody pots
and freedom is sown
with the seeds of valiant men
The harvest is bitter for the settlers and now,
the last exodus gathers frenzy.

The trail points Southward
to the last outpost
(a haven to their whiteness).

And like elephants,
sensing the final hour
they hurry to the sacred sand
(our conquered land)

But let them come
O let the white elephants draw near!

What would be their refuge
Will yet become
Their Dying Ground …

*pen name

from: **black trial**
Ingoapele Madingoane

man the coward
has disowned himself
the rights given to him
by nature
and adopted the fake romance
of self

how i hate the deceitful paradise
that man lives within
and the selfish way he now handles my life

i blew my horn to raise the alarm
and he told me that's no right way
to save us both
i beat the drum
and he loosened the cowhide to stifle the beat
so i left him and wandered alone
in the black forest and asked myself
what in fact does man want

i resigned from paradise
and went back home to africa
in search of my image
to dig up the roots
and burn incense
to strengthen my stand
speaking to my ancestors
in the ancient language of mankind
i heard the spirits talk back to me

i felt my soul astir as they led me
all the way from a black trial
into the land of sunshine and peace
i heard them say
leap high deprived soul
move faster than yesteryear
and climb the freedom wagon
go man go
blackman go

don't crawl to your future
you are bound to be brave
reach your goal blackman
stand up man   stand up and
go man go
blackman go

drag it off brother man
off your back   it ain't yours
break this damn sucker's chain
drop the burden from your shoulders
move on   brother go
go man go
blackman go

leap higher deprived son
jump the lagoon of dark despair
walk to the point of salvation
blow the horn   raise the alarm
beat the drum and let them dance
go man go
blackman go

go man go
blackman go
turn a new leaf
date this creation
scribble on the soil
a good reflection
up off your backside
and
go man go
blackman go

i talk about me
i am africa
i am the blazing desert yonder
a tall proud grain amidst the sand
egypt my head   the nile my oasis
flow on nile   flow on my life blood
i talk about me
i am africa
i am man
ogun's image
made from the soil
abibiman
thus
i talk about me
for
i am africa

hide and seek i lived
on savanna grasslands
talking freedom
eating salvation

sleeping courage
and
dreaming liberation
for the african soil
thus
i talk about man
i talk about me
for
I am africa

jambo i said as i greeted my father
babari   mzuri sana   as he nodded in agreement
a sign of love and admiration
wewe unatoka wapi he asked me
this question the ageing poor man
not aware he was talking to his long lost son
mimi ninatoka nchini kwa africa kusine
kule kwa azania
kwanini wewe umefika hapa
i said *babu nimekuja kuwona ninyi*
in africa the land of your sons
are you in africa   is that you *mwana*
he asked
yes babu   it is me your son
usema nini he asked me again
hapana maneno i answered
he said
    hail *ogun*
    hail *abibiman*
    land of my sons
    sons of my soil
    bed of my roots

      roots of man
      man   son of africa
      i want you
      back
      back home in africa
      when i lost you
      you were a virgin rich with love
      until they split your loins
      eagle spread and raped you all
      within three centuries
      when they boasted their manhood and
      you abandoned their first child
      in the remote trans
      kei
      oh child   land of my sons
      come back home to africa
come back home azania my child
give up your prodigal life
don't go flirting again
maybe in *bophutamokete*
this time
come child
land of my sons
sons of the soil
bed of my roots
roots of man
man   son of africa
peace in africa will be restored
not because man in africa is black but
because he's suffered under the common enemy
for we in africa will not bring colour
between man and reality

so when I say that don't think
politics will be brought into art
for art is in its own
right above politics   bear in mind
brother whatever you do which is not harmful
to the community
has an artistic message of use to the society
and yourself
remember
africa's pride can be expressed in many ways
your face with music
        your pain with music
                your joy with music
and of course your artistic gift
is as important as your presence
wherever the clan gathers so
stick to them brother because
every man is no man without
the structure of his culture
      so beautifully created
      that black natural gift
      from the mould of the african womb
      pity the day it rots
      in the traditional african tomb

it has been my wish and still is my wish
that   whatever happens between me and africa   when we
                                                          part ways
it will not be through cowardice   or should i say
betrayal of my beloved fatherland

i would be glad if i could be buried like a true african
of african definition
> when i take my soul
> to its destination
> when the gong of departure
> reaches my eardrum
> and the cloud of death dominates my eye

wrap me safely
with the hide of an african ox
i will be glad
deliver me to the ancestral village
cast no flowers on my soil
i am an african   as for beauty
i never had a chance to admire it 'cause
africa was not free
i will join the masses that went before me
and as one we shall fight
the ancestral war until justice
is done

The Question
Themba ka Miya

We sat in patches of doom
        Discussing Eternity
All victimised by the question why

Why is Time the undisputed ruler
Why Time rules the minds of madness
Why Time rules from the womb to the tomb
Time that stretches the nerves of my past and cracks the skull
   of my
        future
Time, Time, Time!
You struck your hateful gong
        and hurried the City typist
        for her date with Adam
Who accepted the apple without dispute
        that gave birth to a man/child
Who was swallowed by a slimy polluted
        stream of a life system,

Involved without choice
We saw him reared in an existence of filth
We saw his body smeared in dung of extortion
We saw him listed on a tableau written in his own blood
We saw him in a world painted white, sucking from a love-starved
     system – caressing the doom of domination
We saw them bashing up his skull
        and eating his brains and imagination
        Symbol of Capitalism

We saw him trying to laugh only to end up sobbing
> At 16 he went and lost his name for a number
> At No. 80 Albert Str.

Who lamented in chains protest in his bondage and thereafter gave
> unopposed his gift of hate back handing to the unsociable
>> society

Who was taught the pros and cons of turning the other cheek to the
> holy spirits bottled for Doornkop Cemetery (Pty) Limited

Who rushed to beg for manhood to reach the havens of ten rand a week,
> brandishing a flickering torch, chasing an evasive shadow of
>> hope

Who was seen munching pig style, the vomit left-overs purchased at a
> 'Whites Only' restaurant while sitting on the pavement of
>> highway Jo'burg

Who turned to church and was told God is away on holiday

Who turned to surrender to the bantustans and was seen holding a
> baby dying of malnutrition

Who hung on until they told him that the cow did jump over the moon

Who turned to SASO and was told, 'Black man you are on your own'

Who turned to himself and saw human excrement and ended
> concluding the world is a prison

Who was later arrested crying, and charged for section 6
Who was seen in racist farms dressed to kill in potato sacks,
   his back
       bleeding from the whip of hate
Who walked down the withering limbs of his last discarded
   house
       and was later seen brandishing an okapi in soul-
   destroying
       Soweto
Whose father followed him into grandfather night trying to
   tell him
       what Time it was
       He followed as he watched helplessly his son's youth
   dribbling
       away as he staff-rode the soul train towards ancestral
   damnation
Whose father begged and screamed as he followed through the
   undertakers
       of blood-robotted streets of White City Jabavu
       Through Nip an' Two Beers accompanied by girls from
       Los-my-cherie drinking the blood of the loveless
       Through prisons of vengeance where the matjietas
   blom
He followed scraping his son's sperm dripping from gushing and
       torn wombs of Afrika Motherhood.
He followed, tired, with two great holes of poverty mocking him
       from the bottom of his shoes and found
His hope lay bleeding on the rubble of a slum clearance
At the funeral: the father wore black
       the mother wore black

                    the priest wore black
                    the people wore black
They all cursed their blackness.
O victory put on your coat we are losing the battle to stay alive.

Soul's Disparity
Motlase Mogotsi

We came from faraway,
    from a land of darkness and continuous wars;
Where light seemed very strange to watch,
    the roads there were dangerous with dongas
        gaping at the sun.

When shall we see the sun again
    in this droning night resistant to sleep?
And caress the warm breeze
    from seas of fraternity and love?

We felt western belief
    embracing change in our sleep
We drank this to our fill
    and now we have our eyes glued on the moon!

O, how we sheltered our heads
    under roofs of civilisation …
And froze our hopes in regrets
    for having allowed poor souls to practice an
        alien life!

But every day, when civilisation enlightens our souls,
    we drag our feet in despair …

Old Homes
David Moja-Mphuso

the sun showing the place every morning,
Where every reflection of our eyes
is attracted to our ancestors,
their deeds destined to become memorials of today.
If only we could, unashamed, place those cornerstones again
to be our stepping stones,
discipline carried from mother's knee,
learned there, the family
and all to be the sand of the same
home, with all the branches again
of the same heart.
Why not the body of the land forever
like the ruins of Zimbabwe,
Why not my rooigrond living on
the spirits of our ancestors buried there?
While false beliefs like glue
hold our new homes together …

Our Immortal Mother
Molahlehi wa Mmutle

My mother died a servant
She was buried a meid
A house meid she was
Like a dienskneg she lived
With all humanity removed

On a plank bed she slept
Supported by four Gokoks
Wrapped in a shoal of bags
Covered with rags from her Missies
Radiance of colour and design faded

She scrubbed the floors
Washed their underwear
Like a soulless brute she worked
She had no soul they said
Was she not born to suffer

She ate out of a broken plate
Drank from a cup without handle
Those were oorskiets and krummels
From her divine master's table
Were they not destined to be Masters?

My armsalige Moeder
Sy was te goed om te lewe
Te eerlik vir die wêreld
Mag die Almagtige haar seën
Haar trane, haar bloed lewe

Like a servant she was rewarded
With oud klere and huisraad
She had a Sunday off
To pray and thank their God
For their godheid and genade

They killed her
She died in solitude
Broken – broken to the bone
Without raising an eye to heaven
For the foreign God betrayed her

She lives on in her shrine
Her soul they could not destroy
She went to rest, a goddess,
Worshipped by those she loved
Immortalised by her children

Death
Es'kia Mphahlele

You want to know?
My mother died at 45
at 42 my brother followed.
You want to know?
She cleaned the houses of white folk,
and washed their bodily dirt
out of the baths.
One night a coma took her,
and he –
cancer hounded him two years
and rolled him in the dust.
You want to know?
My grandma left at 80,
she also washed her years away
and saw them flow
into the drain
with the white man's scum.
Many more from our tree have fallen –
known and unknown.

… and that white colossus
he was butchered by a man
they say is mad.

How often do I dream
my dearest dead stand across a river –
small and still I cannot traverse
to join them
and I try to call to them

and they wave and smile so distantly
receding beyond the water
that pulls me in
and spits me out into the dawn of the living.

... and he was butchered
like a buffalo
after overseeing many a negro's execution.

You want to know –
why do I say all this?
what have they to do with us
the ones across the water?
How should I know?
These past two decades
death has been circling closer
and beating the air about me
like a flight of vultures
in a cruel age
when instruments of torture
can be found with any fool and tyrant,
churchman, all alike,
all out to tame the heretic, they say.

... and they tell us
when the colossus fell
he did not even have a triple-worded
Roman chance

And so to kill a bug
they set a house on fire
to kill a fire

they flood a country
to save a country
drench the land in blood
to peg the frontiers of their colour madness
they'll herd us into ghettoes
jail us
kill us slowly
because we are the Attribute
that haunts their dreams
because *they* are the blazing neon lights
that will not let us be
because we are the children of their Sin
they'll try to erase the evidence
because their deeds are howling from a fog
beyond their reach.

… and we laughed and danced
when news came of the death of that colossus
– the death of a beast of prey.

What can we do with the ashes of a tyrant?
who will atone?
whose blood will pay for those of us who went
down under the tanks of fire?
And voices cried It's not enough,
a tyrant dead is not enough!
Vengeance is mine and yours and his,
says the testament of man
nailed to the boulder of pain.

… and they say the butcher's mad
who sank the knife into the tyrant's neck

while the honourable men
who rode his tanks of fire
looked on
as if they never heard of giants die
as they had lived,
and all about the frog who burst
when he pushed his energy
beyond the seams of his own belly.

What if I go as the unknown solider
or attended by a buzzing fly?
what if my carcass were soaked in organ music,
or my ancestors had borne me home?
I hear already
echoes from a future time of voices
coming from a wounded bellowing multitude
cry Who will atone
Who will atone?

You want to know? –
because I nourish
a deadly life within
my madness shall have blood.

Nineteen Seventy-Six
Oupa Thando Mthimkulu

Go nineteen seventy-six
We need you no more
Never come again
We ache inside.
Good friends we have
Lost.
Nineteen seventy-six
You stand accused
Of deaths
Imprisonments
Exiles
And detentions.
You lost the battle
You were not revolutionary
Enough
We do not boast about you
Year of fire, year of ash.

Ngwana wa Azania
a proemdra for oral delivery
Mothobi Mutloatse

– The future of the black child, the recalcitrant Azanian child in South Africa, is as bright as night and this child, forever uprooted, shall grow into a big sitting duck for the uniformed gunslinger.
– From ages two to four he shall ponder over whiteness and its intrigue. From ages five to eight he shall prise open his jacket-like ears and eyes to the stark realisation of his proud skin of ebony. From ages nine to fifteen he shall harden into an aggressive victim of brainbashing and yet prevail. From ages sixteen to twenty-one he shall eventually graduate from a wavering township candle into a flickering life-prisoner of hate and revenge and hate in endless fury. This motherchild shall be crippled mentally and physically for experimental purposes by concerned quack statesmen parading as philanthropists.
– This motherchild shall be protected and educated free of state subsidy in an enterprising private business asylum by Mr Nobody. This motherchild shall mother the fatherless thousands and father boldly the motherless million pariahs. This nkgonochild shall recall seasons of greed and injustice to her war-triumphant and liberated Azachilds. This mkhuluchild shall pipesmoke in the peace and tranquillity of liberation, and this landchild of the earth shall never be carved up ravenously again and the free and the wild and the proud shall but live together in their original own unrestricted domain without fear of one another, and this waterchild shall gaily bear its load without a fuss like any other happy mother after many suns and moons of fruitlessness in diabolical inhumanity.
– This gamble-child of zwêpe shall spin coins with his own

delicate life to win the spoils of struggle that is life itself. This child of despair shall shit in the kitchen; shit in the lounge, shit in the bedroom-cum-lounge-cum-kitchen; he shall shit himself dead; and shall shit everybody as well in solidarity and in his old-age shall dump his shit legacy for the benefit of his granny-childs: this very ngwana of redemptive suffering; this umtwana shall but revel in revealing off-beat, creative, original graffiti sugar-coated with sweet nothings like:

re tlaa ba etsa power/re-lease Mandela/azikhwelwa at all costs/we shall not kneel down to white power/release Sisulu/jo' ma se moer/black power will be back tonight/release or charge all detainees/msunuwakho/down with booze/Mashinini is going to be back with a bang/to bloody hell with bantu education/ don't shoot — we are not fighting/Azania eyethu/masende akho/majority is coming soon/freedom does not walk it sprints/ inkululeko ngoku!

– This child born in a never-ending war situation shall play marbles seasonably with TNTs and knife nearly everyone in sight in the neighbourhood for touch and feel with reality, this child of an insane and degenerated society shall know love of hatred and the eager teeth of specially-trained biting dogs and he will speak animatedly of love and rage under the influence of glue and resistance.

– This marathon child shall trudge barefooted, thousands of kilometres through icy and windy and stormy and rainy days and nights to and from rickety church-cum-stable-cum-classrooms with bloated tummy to strengthen him for urban work and toil in the goldmines, the diamond mines, the coal mines, the platinum mines, the uranium mines so that he should survive countless weekly rockfalls, pipe bursts, and traditional faction fights over a meal of maiza that has been recommended for family planning.

– This child of raw indecision and experimentation shall sell

newspapers from street corners and between fast moving cars for a dear living breadwinning instead of learning about life in free and compulsory school, and shall provide the capitalistic country with the cheapest form of slavery the labourglobe has ever known and the governor of the reserve bank shall reward him with a thanks-for-nothing-thanks-for-enriching-the-rich kick in the arse for having flattened inflation alone hands-down.
– This child of the tunnels shall occasionally sleep malunde for an on-the-spot research into the effects of legalised separation of families and he shall find his migrant long-lost father during a knife-duel in a men's hostel and his domestic mother shall he ultimately embrace passionately in a cul de sac in the kitchen in a gang-bang.
– This child of concrete shall record and computerise how the boss shouts and swears publicly at his heroically shy father-boy and how the madam arrogantly sends his mother-girl from pillar to bust. He shall photograph how the superior doctor addresses his unkempt mother in untailored talk as if mother-stupid had conceived a baboon-child.
– This observant child shall taste its first balanced meal in an i.c.u., and in the very intensive care unit shall he be revived to further life and misery and malnutrition in this immensely-wealthy land to loosen up the bones down to their perforated marrow.
– This child of the donga shall watch in jubilation and ecstasy and ire as its godforsaken, godgiven home called squatter camp is razed through its permission down to the ground by demolishing bulldozers lately referred to as front-enders.
– This child of nowhere shall of his own free will join the bandwagon and ravaza its own Botshabelo to lighten the merciless soil conservationists' burden for a place in the sun of uncertainty, he shall show absolute respect for his elders with a

hard kierie blow across the grey head and shall be unanimously nominated for a nobel peace prize for his untold, numerous contributions to human science at a local mortuary.
– This child born into a callous and too individualistically-selfish society shall be considered sane until further notice by psychopaths masquerading as men of law. He shall be an unmatched hero with an undecided following, having paralysed parents and preachers alike with his frankness and willingness not only to whisper nor speak about wanting to be free but to bloody well move mountains to be free!
– This child of evictions shall sleep in toilets while its off-spring cross the borders for possible m.t.
– This child of rags to rags and more rags to riches school uniform tatters shall quench his thirst with dishwater in the suburbs and also with methylated spirits in the deadendstreet camps to communicate with the gods.
– This child shall breastfeed her first baby before her seventeenth birthday and be highly pleased with motherhood lacking essential fatherhood. This child of uneasiness shall trust nobody, believe in no one, even himself, except perhaps when he's sober. This ghettochild shall excel in the pipi-olympics with gold and bronze medals in raping grannies with every wayward erection and eviction from home resulting from ntate's chronic unemployment and inability to pay the hovel rent.
– This growing child of the kindergarten shall psychologically avoid a school uniform admired telegraphically by uniformed gunfighters of maintenance of chaos and supremacy. He shall smother moderation goodbye and throttle reason in one hell of a fell swoop, and the whole scheming world shall cheer him up to the winning post with its courage in the mud and its heart in its pink arse. This child of dissipation shall loiter in the shebeen in earnest search for its parents and shall be battered and abused to

hell and gone by its roving parents when reunited in frustration in an alleyway.
– This child of bastardised society and bastard people-in-high-office and colour-obsession of paranoid of communism and humanism, shall break through and snap the chain of repression with its bare hands, and this child, with its rotten background and slightly bleak future shall however liberate this nuclear crazy world with Nkulunkulu's greatest gift to man: ubuntu.
– This lambschild shall remind the nation of the oft-remembered but never-used ISINTU:

Mangwana o tshwara thipa ka fa bogaleng.

In this World, my Sister
Nthambeleni Phalanndwa

I

It all started in the church
We looked each other in the eyes
Your devastating smile
Yes, it made me forget reality
My mind a radio
Playing two stations at a time
And I listened to both
The faint voice of the preacher
And the sweet loud voice
Conveyed by your smile.

The preacher continued to talk
While I sat there
Like a fly to be swallowed by a frog
So innocently in love
And people started to sing
While from another world
I heard them faintly from afar.

We became correspondents for a year
Me writing sweet letters to you
You writing sweeter ones in return
And we were happy and grateful
For that was friendship
But even so
Visit each other we could not
I had no money
And you had no time.

Correspondence continued
Until you had to ask
As I continued to write
Calling you darling sometimes
Without calling it a spade
Then I poured it all out
All I felt at the church
The first time we met
And in reply you said:
'The best evidence
of our love
Is not a long letter
Or something big
It is the little things
That we do day by day
that best say
I LOVE YOU.'
On that Saturday you came
where I used to dwell
All day long
We sat on the bricks
We caressed, kissed and cried

For it was sweet
With veins like copper conductors
In which flew electrons of love
Mouths serving as a switch
And the circuit was complete
Both benumbed
We sat there
And forgot
That we had no chair.

In the evening when I cooked
You sat on those bricks
Unconcerned,
Loving me.
After we had eaten
You congratulated me
On the delicious food I cooked
And it was night.
After reading you some poems
You asked for water
To wash your face and feet
I looked at your bare torso
And saw your pointed breasts so proud.

We got between the blankets
Two on the floor
And one on us
Again
You never complained.

For a month you went on leave
You neither wrote nor came
You later wrote to tell why
It was due to heavy rains
That left the people homeless and starving.

II

My dear J,
These things do happen in the lives of men
That sons and daughters
Are separated from their parents

Husbands separated from their wives
And during such times
We sit down
Balance our heads between our hands
Look into the skies
We see the future bleak.

We feel our legs go lame
Our hearts dead within our bodies
Fear-stricken people
Living in deadly fear of a knock on the door
For who knows
You may be next
To leave your next of kin.

But this, I will not discuss
Lest I bring down
The wrath of heaven and earth on my head
I leave it as a legend
For fathers to tell their children one day.

Only memories fill my mind now
I am empty of love
Hate is what I see
Written all over people's faces
Carving furrows that make them look like scarecrows.

The dead are dead my sister
We cannot ask them questions
The living must answer
They must tell us all we want to know
They must tell us now

For in this world my sister
No more
No more can I go on seeking
Justice, fairness and truth
These things do not exist.

I tried to walk
And stopped along the way
The signboard was dumb
I didn't know which road to take
I just stood and gazed
But the signboard did not tell
Only in my memories of the past
I saw a man playing an accordion in church.

But there in church
The congregation waited and hoped
But the priest did not come
And there at school
Students to write exams within a fortnight
With half of the syllabus still undone
Waited for their history teacher with hope
But the teacher did not come.

I want to suggest
That we go into the bushy mountains
And see if baboons are caged
Let's go to the seas
And see if fishes no longer swim
Perhaps we shall understand
That the change has come
Through the will of

GOD
THE SON
AND THE HOLY GHOST

You gods of Africa
And you my father I do not blame you
But you never told me
That the sun rises and sets
That flowers bloom and wither
That this world grows thorny trees
That prick the feet
I have been burnt
I now dread the fire
My heart wails
It keeps on bleeding
The wounds are deep
Big gashes left there
By the broken pieces of …

At least
Beyond the distant horizon
The sun still shines
        THERE
        NOW
I want to go THERE
        NOW
Go quietly THERE
        NOW
Speak to nobody
Address the winds
Greet my friends the immortal boulders
Mortal beings can force you to hate
And hate and hate …

But when you have an aim in life
It is like travelling in a tunnel
The darkness worries you not
The little light at the other end
Is comfort enough to kill your bitterness.

Right now
I bid you farewell my sister
People do meet and part
Children get born
Some die young … these are fortunate
But on the thoroughfare of life
Let's both go our separate ways
I want to toddle out of this limbo
Up until I cross the Limpopo
Alone.

Then I will start my march
Until I cross the River Congo
And if not dead with fatigue
I will reach Cameroon
To meet Mbella Sonne Dipoko
I want to meet him and ask
If he knows what they do in the veld.

Then I will continue my march
Until my destination is reached
And here
I want to talk to Cyprian Ekweni
Have lunch with Chinua Achebe
And I will ask them
If they know the veld

I want to tell them
That there
Baboons do eat mealies during the night
Then they will write
And the world shall know
What is happening in the veld
And on their advice
I will settle down
And learn at Ibadan.

No more turning back
I have seen enough of the veld
Where our lives are not our own.

My Name
Nomgqibelo Ncamisile Mnqhibisa
Magoleng wa Selepe

Look what they have done to my name …
the wonderful name of my great-great-grandmothers
Nomgqibelo Ncamisile Mnqhibisa

The burly bureaucrat was surprised
What he heard was music to his ears
'Wat is daai, sê nou weer?'
'I am from Chief Daluxolo Velayigodle of emaMpodweni
And my name is *Nomgqibelo Ncamisile Mnqhibisa.*'

Messia, help me!
My name is so simple
and yet so meaningful,
but to this man it is trash …

He gives me a name
Convenient enough to answer his whim:
I end up being
Maria …
I …
Nomgqibelo Ncamisile Mnqhibisa.

We the Dancers
Eugene Skeef

We the dancers
Greeted the sun
Sitting by the lowest step
Of the curtained house
We were the old nurse
For the faded child
See the way we felt
In the blueness of her eye
We will sit
Before the house was built
We will drink our tears
Before her eye could blink
When we will dance
We were free …

We the dancers
Came dead with the fetching flame
We were the fly
The fires feared
Yet took for our wings' release
We waited as the bars
Held in cell window-sills
For the off-beat
We will slip
Before the count was expected
When we will fly
The sun was borne in our pinion …

We the dancers
Awoke the bare earth
To yield to the tattoo
Our temper beat
The senile moth moulted
Beyond the strains of the nocturne
Our lowered foot
Quivered at the ordination
Of an apprenticed midwife
Far from the African wharf
Oblivious of its prophetic poise
Even the squeak
Of the lower deck
Could not shame the resonance
Of the sibilant silence
Of our bearing wave
The minor cadence of our song
Groaning aloft the Atlantic storm
As we dance to go
To become loose
In the flesh of the apple
We will skin too the serpent
Before the earth wore trees
Men we will move
The waters have 'brought forth
Abundantly the moving creatures
That have life …'

Custodian of our Spirit
Farouk Stemmet

oh Baobab
you stand firm
in the soil
in which you always stood
you stand firm
in the soil
in which you will always stand

your wrinkled bark testifies
to a memory
rich in times and events
long forgotten by man

you are not the rolling tide
you are not the changing cloud
you are neither the weeping willow
nor the departing ibis
you are not fallible man

you have never been colonised
you have always belonged
to the soil in which you stand

though your branches
may be chopped and pruned
you remain yourself
for your roots are secure
in the soil
which gave you birth

though your trunk is wide
and exposed to much
you can shield many

though the air about you may change
you will live forever

'Oh Africa seek your Spirit in me'

Wooden Spoon
K Zwide

I carved a spoon from a rose-root
and, though thornless, its shape was strange,
conforming with the twisted nature
of the rose's journey into the earth.

Grandfather carved a straight spear
of a fine yellow wood;
melted ironstone with oxfat
and beat the blade on a rock,
and, blessing it with leaves and milk,
he whirled it into the air.
In response to gravity
it pierced his heart.

Now I eat with a crooked spoon
which I have dug from my master's garden
and it pierces my heart.

A Riot Policeman
Christopher van Wyk

The sun has gone down
with the last doused flame.
Tonight's last bullet
has singed the day's last victim
an hour ago.
It is time to go home.

The hippo crawls
in a desultory air of triumph
through, around fluttering
shirts and shoes full of death.
Teargas is simmering.

Tears have been dried by heat
or cooled by death.
Buckshot fills the space
between the maimed and the mourners.
It is time to go home.

A black man surrenders
a stolen bottle of brandy
scurries away with his life
in his hands.
The policeman rests the oasis
on his lips
wipes his mouth on a camouflaged
cuff.
It is time to go home.

Tonight he'll shed his uniform.
Put on his pyjamas.
Play with his children.
Make love to his wife.
Tomorrow is pay-day.
But it is time to go home now,
It is time to go home.

Present Day

john 1:1 and me
Lebohang Masango

No matter what version of the sky you know
there are as many words as there are stars in the galaxy.
The gift presents in cosmic abundance
an endless assemblage of master keys.
Words unlock language and language, a new world.
The doors of possibility burst open
when the alphabet is merged.

Imaginations are colourful canvases:
How you write sing speak dance
brushstrokes of creativity;
How you relinquish power to our senses
To believe in the magic created
when you close your eyes to see.
And as it goes, what can ever shroud your dreams,
when all that surrounds you
is brought into existence by
the very words you speak?

And we have always been a story people:
we carry the praise poetry of our surnames
like ancient geography
a composite map of our present selves
charting ancestral triumphs.
It is through our daily breath and deeds
that we remix and remaster this mythology.
This inheritance reminds us that
though we may be found wanting and weak,

along with every god and genius that has ever been,
we too are capable of the greatness that we seek.

South Africa is part glorious beauty
and part ravenous beast.
Its worst fragments
feeding on the murky darkness
of our collective actions.
It is a nation compelled to fly right
yet look backwards
to unsettle the gaze and reflect beyond the surface.
So even when we struggle to hold a mirror up to its flaws,
this act of constant reflection calls to the light
and illuminates a truth of healing purpose.

And we have always been a story people:
Our fathers chanted their protests against the sky,
yearned for change come down like rain to bless us.
Our mothers swallowed their prayers
deep into their wounded parts,
pleaded that they would move like mercy to heal us.
Our elders spoke their words like medicine unto each other,
uttered courage and compassion to soothe us,
Themselves, a people who knew how a hell
made by the world could dwell
inside you intimately.
They, broken but hoping, cradled the dawn for a joy
more certain than the violence of mourning.

And what can never be denied,
we are the very best thing that can happen
when imagination dares to fly.

To every birth, its blood: we are the pots of gold
finally realised beneath South Africa's rainbow sign.
We are the ones;
we are the fire this time.

clots of blood
Vangile Gantsho
after Hiromi Itō 'Coyote'

My grandmother was a teacher
My mother was a healer
My mother's younger sister was a Christian
My mother's other younger sister had a paralysed daughter
All were wonderfully beautiful.

When I was born, my grandmother sent a telegram with
    my name.
She saw me in a dream.
My grandmother saw herself reborn through my mother.
When I left home, after she had died
She visited me in a dream.
Painted three dots from blood onto my forehead.

My mother birthed four children.
Her second son took too much of her blood into his heart.
When my brother died in her arms
My mother could not heal him.
When I was born, two years after, my mother had stopped
    healing.
All her faith clotted inside my lungs.
I didn't cry when I was born.
My mother held me silent, for thirty minutes in her arms.
When the nurse tried to pry me away from her,
My grandmother's telegram arrived.
My mother says I laughed when the nurse tried to take me
    from her.
She birthed two children after failing to heal her second son.

My mother was a believer.
My grandmother was a healer.
My mother's younger sister was a Christian.
My mother's other younger sister had a paralysed daughter.
All were wonderfully beautiful.

My mother's younger sister's paralysed daughter died when
    she was fifteen.
My mother's younger sister visited her on the other side.
When her daughter returned,
after three months inside a mechanical heartbeat
she had three clots of blood down the front of her body,
On her chest, in her navel, just above her vagina.
She still could not walk.

My grandmother was touched by her father's younger brother.
My mother was touched by her mother's sister's husband.
My mother's younger sister was also touched by her mother's
    sister's husband.
My mother's other younger sister was touched by her mother's
    uncle.
My mother had always wanted a daughter.
She never left me alone with any of her sisters' husbands.

The protection my mother gave me
Was The Bible, fear and chastity.
We were all afraid of God, men, and the dark.

Black Beauty
Katleho Kano Shoro

Black Beauty:
Beautifully Black.
Black Gift:
Gifted Black.

Gifted and Black,
Young, Gifted and Black,
Gifted but Young.

Black beautifully Young,
Black always Young.
Black too Young.
Black too Beautiful.
Beauty too Black.

Black fades to Black.

Is Black beautiful too?
Is Black beauty beautiful too?
Is Black youth a gift?
A beautiful gift?

born(e) to the grave
Mjele Msimang

i may have been born on 27 April 1994 –
but i was never born free.

as long as we pay homage to statues
of colonial laws that decided how bodies
language
their own love,
i was never born free

as long as my dress
hisses snake-like in a man's temple
when it's wound round my hips,
i was never born free

as long as we forget how memory
is in the tooth of a flower that
does not seed when we only know
its beauty in latin,
i was never born free

as long as we fool ourselves that
an African nation on the Security Council
means liberation,
i was never born free

as long as the icc's neck is kept
on amerikkka's leash, its snout
twitching
for the scent of African leaders –
i was never born free

as long as governments strum happy harps
of loveless austerity to quieten
the iridescent rage
of justice,
i was never born free

as long as this government pays
the imf's penny for the apartheid
piper that paupered these coffers,
i was never born free

as long as governments exist
then the ballot is the bullet
we were never born free

as long as this land is wreathed
in mandible & jaw beneath
sidewalks, metatarsal & femur
scattered along reaching hills,
unable to decompose for they are nameless,
we were never born free

as long as this land's people
know it as a tin shack from which
they must pick grapes & fold clothes
under a white sun,
we were never born free

as long as we do not stretch our bloods
across
borders fashioned by men who believed themselves gods,
we were never born free

as long as there is not a day to lament at the foot
of the
Atlantic
wail our pain into that long watery hell
for souls that crossed & never came back
–
we were never born free

as long as the curriculum is a coffin
of colonial love
poems,*
we were never born free

as long as this country exists
(as long as you do not understand)
as long as this country exists
(as long as we are ash)
as long as this country exists
(as long as we are disremembered)
as long as this country exists

> then my children & your children
> will never be born free
> will be born(e) to the grave

---

* See Natalie Diaz's 'Postcolonial Love Poem' in: Diaz, Natalie. *Postcolonial Love Poem*: Graywolf Press, 2020.

jol'iinkomo
David wa Maahlamela

I

jol'iinkomo! jol'iinkomo! the herder has been forgotten
   we cried   red-eyed as
 we got off the ride of trashed pride
we read and trekked dark yet compelling pugs of your essential
   disturbance
words jolting blinkered horses   driving stolen cattle back to the
   black kraal
 words undeceiving apes
   words that do not bite their own tails or tongues when they
     divulge the future
the humpty-dumpty's great fall.   poetry of two sights
   and four eyes
     amplifying literary canon   that thing murmured by biko
   and fanon.

we read your poems read you inside-out at the reading in your
   honour
you only spoke through ears gave an ear to your many selves
our gifts to you were the cattle we stole from your own kraal
like vultures around a carcass we gossiped with you about you

some poems enjoyable because they are not understandable
some melodic because they do not sing
some seductive because they stripped off metaphoric miniskirts
lure so pure and unclad, bare-knuckled with no jockstrap
no make-believe   no makeshift   words skinny-dipping
carpet-bombing margins   blending othering with brothering

poetry that electrifies the squatter camp and electrocutes the
   suburb
hammarsdale to Havana   verulam to vietnam
others scrawl endemics   you wax epidemics
you give rap swagger, the old teaching new how to be new
   (new is old forgotten)
short punch-rhymes of long sting vocal painting words surfing
   and skating
not in any way but in the best way, not tolerably well but
   intolerably better
poetry of engagement not disengaged from artistic beauty.

II

mafika   he whose arrival is noticeable   mafika with
   bullet-stones wrapped in words
mafika   the sharpshooter no accidental that   gwala
   rhymes with bala   your writing nails
ignorance to the cross   shoots sense straight to the soul
   blues beyond lamentation
    serenade under the tropical jacket of blood   jeremiad
   of a jacana on a jacaranda
      some people are born for it   some it
   was born for them.

your poetry is the   uncontainable
      the   untameable and
     the   ungovernable at its best
crumbs of   undone love of this turbulent society
of paper ogres saturated with plastic arrogance.

baba gwala   you gave soundscape meaning
your poetry doesn't cuddle pain or coddle rain
it doesn't strike bows to the plain for the rainbow notion
you write disturbed cobra   confluence of shashe and limpopo
    that cut
than sharp blade of colour-joint at the cape point.

III

the hunter   you said   shall be hunted
    today the hunted mimics tunes of the hunter
    poets are pets choked by bow-ties of modesty
    for their vice-ridden leaders politicians are ready to kill
    the only public art of these days
    is the eating of sushi on human bodies
    what used to be poetry is now written under shades of
shame and fear
    poets' abashed conscience stares at them with its tail
knotted.
till when will we turn the other cheek?

your colubrine friends baba give you glassy eyes
as they belch drinks of names they cannot pronounce
when they meet you in corridors they cover faces with gizmos
josephs are always curs sold by their own   if not killed   ask hani
langa sobukwe ushaka sekhukhune makhado ramabulana
it is not a sauna room but ozone layer melting down.
who dare tells poetic pets of orchards and ochres that
a nation without silver-tongued poets
is but a political limousine
cruise-controlled on a high way of corruption?

'poetry of insurrection   grind your sharp-tongue
censorship is abolished but we remain the valve station
we do not censor nor jail we just shut all your valves
watch you radicalising on a quicksand of despair
we will repaint the new state of poetry before you
idolise a monopoly of tongue-tamed mediocre
to breed the next generation of poetic pets.'
undeniably there is a new old in our land.

the quest for reclaiming the lost
or guarding the endangered is torturous
we are bitten by the same wall you tried to bite down
same mosquito bites you defied
same limitations and unfitness of language
along the way the honest run out of juice.
your poetry captures death in the most lively of ways.

IV

your demise was already written on the thick palm of
    grahamstown winter
 your shadow was still with us but its threads pulled at the other
    end of eden's groove
 your shadow was no longer walking by your side but rather
    before you
winter drizzles were beginning to erase your mystique and pugs.

                   your
                         unmistakable voice
                                    only spoke
                                             in silence.

was your heart giggling and scampering in this premature
    memorial of an inhaling shade?
ours is a country far   far from beauty
                     a country beautiful
          beautiful from far.

V

death does not begin with the last pulse of the heartbeat
you said   neither does it end with the doctor's certificate
you died for many years
oom matthews told me of the visit he paid you
in one of your many deaths
each death erased you from our country's memory
this country baba is far from beauty but beautiful afar
country of see-saw love in which towers of integrity fall
poets are political affiliations reciting polling stations.
viral sex-tape of kafka's ape a victim of moral rape.
time is panacea, the wall the fool's writing pad.

at least your soul was still factory packaged
we celebrated you two months before your last
even though with but a flight ticket and stipend
at least you did not throw yourself out of a skyscraper
or out of a moving train or into the gravy train of agitprops
l.k.j. was also honoured here with an honorary doctorate
deem yourself favoured to be honoured   ((sadly, with your
    own words!)).
papa rams says words are medicine which is to mean also poison.
in these inhumanities of the faculty of humanities you never
allowed the belly to outbalance the brain

your words never curtsied to any strain.
you outfaced the faceless
to the bitter end.

now that you are gone   have you ceased dying?

Citizen Minus
Khadija Heeger

Suffering has a black skin.
How am I to be now that I am made of glass
and words have no sound except for those uttered in a past?
Sometimes I'm black
when politics parodies a truth and quantity is king.
Sometimes I am black.
Sometimes only in the vaguest sense do I have a history
a memory, a cultural reality.
Easier to keep me in the dark,
easier to talk about the Indian Ocean slave trade
as if it were one of the stepsisters,
easier to say that I almost suffered
am almost one thing
not quite another.

Somewhere between here and there
between 1994 and the present
I was lost on the periphery of a South African story
because if memory serves the historical themes it seems
my people were never participants in the resistance
never marched, never fought, never died.

Coloured anomaly
forcibly removed, survivors of slave ancestry
the sum total of my past coined thus
and by degree I'm the not so bad-off progeny.
'We won't omit you completely, we'll just play with the lighting
so it won't look so frightening.'
Pieces of a story,

just enough said so you'll go quietly to bed.
Citizen not quite black.

Ek is mos ve'koep dee' my manskap,
'n government wat alwee' praat van equality en freedom
ma hiesie ding: die vinge wys ve'by daa' waa' ek bly,
issie so bad offie,
maakie saak hoeveel gengsters en drug addic's daa'issie.

It kommie vannie strugglie
and is by definition not defined as an apartheid crime.
Citizen wassie daa' nie, maggie kla nie
vrek van pille roek met 'n apartheid spoek.

And now 18 years later, left with a democratic hangover
and a negotiated new South Africa,
I find that 'not an apartheid crime' ruining the length and
    breadth
of mostly coloured youth
filling the gap between yesterday and today
with a smell not unlike that of the
underdog.
Unity in diversity becomes a travesty if we omit just one you see
but history it seems is a commodity
something dressed for a particular emphasis
sold to the appropriate buyer.
'But it's not that simple,' they tell me, 'there are complexities
if you please, don't over-simplify!'
Is it complex to lie, make over, storyboard, edit
till you don't see the ones slipping through the cracks?
Until suffering has one colour and prosperity another?
And I become the pain you see through

now that I am made of glass
and the skeleton of my ancestors can be seen in the faces of the young?

We carve a dubious future at best
but I like a ghost will not rest
until equal means what it is
and recognition is fair
and suffering has no colour;
until I have no more gooseflesh in these modern day prisons
    of freedom
for all
where we create more underdogs for the next struggle.

Hoekoo' gat o's daa' in 'nni blinddoek vasgevang
gemang dee 'n fucked up understanding of identity?
Hoe vê' aluta, hoe vê' continua?
Ek is mos ve'koep dee' my manskap,
'n government wat alwee' praat van equality en freedom
ma hiesie ding: die vinge wys ve'by daa' waa' ek bly,
issie soe bad offie, maakie saak
hoeveel gengsters en drug addic's daa' issie.
It kommie vannie strugglie
and is by definition not defined as an apartheid crime.
Citizen wassie daa' nie, maggie kla nie
vrek van pille roek met 'n apartheid spoek.

A love poem to the 'Problematic' Black Womxn
Puleng Lange Stewart

Aggressive?
No. she said

Undressing her in
her sixth tongue
redressing her with
bland understandings of
unilingualisms
which have never truly
acknowledged the
five other skins
wrapped
snugly around her ability
to create meaning

Instead:
Young and
Black and
Female and
Loud
quicktime translate into Aggression
belying the intricate
complexities which
weave together the
inflections of her Xhosa
intonations of her Phedi
the imperatives of her Shangane
all squeezed into the
eloquence of her English

see
she knows her privilege
when she speaks
words with none of the
Long Elongated
vowels
no-one else seems able to say
without (sub)consciously
making fun

Aggressive?
asked the girl
with long natty locks
and a Biko gospel
No – Passionate
about those
uncomfortable English words
The loud ones
The impolite ones that
challenge a status quo which
keeps the other
five tongues in
cages
flicking the one you'll
listen to in
shapes that
conjure up images of
an abandoned revolution
the body count of monopolized
social 'evolutions'

Aggressive? No
Angry

she says
and far less than
she should be
or could be
because look beneath you
you're still standing on
the same land
: For Now
living lives built on stolen
time

'My mother was a
kitchen-girl
My father was a
Garden-boy
That's why I'm a
Socialist
I'm a Socialist
I'm a Socialist'
she sings
And come
scoff
, please, scoff
and tisk
and click-tongues
Clutch your Pearls
at the palpable
Burning
rage of today
in the wake of a
(not even slightly) 'Bloodless Transition'
still

claiming casualties
And the people shall
share in the
wealth of the land
See –
I understand how
funny this must seem
when it appears outside
a Freedom Charter theme
because
the practicalities of
equality were never
supposed to be so
extreme

Instead:
somewhere …
at some point …
(a few generations down the line)
money will drip down
into the right hands
having
slipped out enough
car windows
to enough car guards
Because the
egalitarian nature of
neo-liberal capitalism
just works that way?
And privilege is
naturally inclined to
give itself up without a fight?

And then – Yes
– young black female –
Be Aggressive
Bare your teeth!
Be the bane of
polite conversation.
Ruin dinner parties,
Lecture theatres,
and all other spaces built
only to tolerate you
with the aggressive
insertion of yourself.
The wholeness of you
the blackness of you
the curve and dip and rage of you
as an extending site of struggle.
Bang at the gates.
Make them all bear witness
to the wounds
so actively unlooked at
Brandish them and say
'I have not forgotten you
and you shall not forget me
through ignoble attempts to
nullify this history'

Be
Aggressive
with those uncomfortable words

Rage in all those tongues

Your Poem Saved Me
Ayanda Billie

In hours of strange dreams
The air was damp and motionless
It felt like the end of the world was near
My forehead touching the sky

In the sky there is a moon,
Her shape stops you
And makes you see yourself
Over the high sea

From where I stand
There is a little girl, dead
Behind Umnga tree
With a yellow dress and one earring

There is a funeral procession every weekend
In Matanzima road
Accompanied by an eternity
Of hot tears

There is non-stop music from the tavern
'Jerusalem ikhaya lam'
Frightening the birds
Tormenting the stillness of the stars

There will be more and more dying
Storm of stars invading the sky
And I remember your poem
Where our people's sorrows are buried.

Untitled poem #1
4 November 2016, 2:47 am
Ashanti Kunene

I joined the revolution because of love
I stayed in the revolution because of love
I left the revolution because of love
But this black revolution refuses to leave me because I love
I cannot separate love from the revolution
Black liberation for me has always been rooted in the ability to fully love and to be loved fully
To love unlovable broken beings that do not think themselves worthy of love
That one showed me my immortality, taught me to have no fear and to see the entire universe within myself.
But this one, this one
He is my spirit.
He is my spirit of defiance.

Izint'eziphukile
Siza Nkosi Mokhele

Hhay' ngob' ngiphuma phakath'
kwezinto eziphukile
ziyachichima izibaya ekhaya
ugog'uzethe zonke ngamagama

Ngelinye ilanga enye yezinkomazi
yaselwa ukubuyel' emzimkhulu
sayizwa ibhonga ngomlomo
muuuumuuuu ayashisa amabele

Ubisi lugcwele, ithole liyafa indlala
ngicela ungivulele salukazi
wavula ugogo lathokoza ithole
lathoba unina ngokuncela

Salekelela nathi ngokuyisenga
saluphuza lufudumele ubisi
hhayi ngoba ngiphuma phakathi'
kwezint' eziphukile

Ngiphuma emanxiweni
emisamo edungwe yizivunguvungu
ezaleni - lapho abadala belinde khona
lapho abafazi beguqa ngamadol'aphukile

Ngibazi kahle ubuhlungu
bokufelw' izinto ozikhonzile
ujeke wezimbali
nesitofu samalahle ska gogo

Broken things
Siza Nkosi Mokhele

not because I emerge out
of broken things
kraals in my homestead are overflowing
grandmother has named them all

one day one of the heifers
was late to return to the great-house
we heard it bellowing
moooo mooo my teats are in heat

there is abundant milk, the calf is emaciated
please let me in old-lady
grandmother opened up to the calf's jubilation
it soothed its mother by suckling

we also assisted by milking it
we drank the milk while it was warm
not because I emerge out
of broken things

I come from maternal quarters
from ancestral altars soiled by whirlwinds
at the hearth – where the elders lie waiting
where women kneel on broken knees

I know pain well
the sorrow of losing that which I held dear
a bowl in which flowers were kept
the coal-stove tales of grandmother

Ngakhiwe ngomlotha
ngiphula izinto yintukuthelo
hhayi ngoba ngiphuma
phakathi kwezint'eziphukile

I am built out of ashes
I break things out of anguish
not because I came from
the midst of broken things

Translated from the Zulu by Menzi Maseko

#FeesMustFall
Zéwande Bk. Bhengu

I am the heir of broken 1994 dreams.
Democracy doesn't know me.
I am still held back by my skin
and the scars of my history.

I am that savage
who still has to beg for education
while you swim in your privilege.
My whole family works fingers to the bone
chasing my certificate.

My feet are anchored in debt.
My destiny is uninhabited.
My body is drenched in sweat.
My economic movement is limited.

So excuse us for disrupting the systems
but we are veteran victims of empty promises.
We are being systematically excluded
using university fee increases.

We will not be silent
while the government propagates economic violence.
Their bodyguards bring in live ammunition
Against young adults and minors.

Remember,
making peace impossible makes violence inevitable.

So call us what you will:
Savages, delinquents, monkeys and preliterates.

We are that generation that stands appalled.
That unrelenting and immovable wall.
We will stand from dusk till dawn.
These fees will fall.

The Forgotten
Sithembiso 'Sthe Khali' Khalishwayo

My name was meant to be 0962785. It was the name I was meant to be given on the first day that I entered through those gates, signed some forms, attached a card to myself, and walked through the hallways of education. Step up from yesterday and enter into today. That day never happened. The gates were closed. They told me that they were fighting for 'Free Education for all'. I think they forgot about me when they shouted from the rooftops. They created a story before my voice was even heard. I guess I have to tell my story to you, if you are willing to listen.

I was born in eDumbe, a small village a few sounds away from Paulpietersburg. I raised cows and chickens, those were my pets. I remember getting my acceptance letter to study at this institution that has many hallways, a card the size of my gogos purse that proves my existence. I was so happy; the kid from a village that never believed in him had finally made it. A few months later, I took a taxi to Joziburg with my gogo, we had about R500 on us to cover everything. R220 to get to Joziburg, R220 to return home, R60 for food.

It was meant to take us one day to register and get that card and go back home. But the voices from the rooftops shouted 'FREE EDUCATION FOR ALL'.

The village was right, I would never make it. The doors were closed before I could enter. So I'll just sit here in my village and take care of my pets.

0666914, that's not my birth name, you gave me that name so I could believe that this house you built would keep me warm during the cold days and feed my desire for this thing that you call education. I see your education for what it is; it doesn't have any foundation to stand on. The fences are low lit with drops of blood running through its seams. I see your neatly trimmed green grass that didn't allow a person, a man like me raised on dirty streets, using a packet of Mabele pap as my pillow. Your house won't allow me in until I clock in and you receive your paycheck. It must be a lucrative business, you didn't create a home, you sold us out and created a hotel so that the rest of the world could admire you from a distance. But I see you, through your tinted glass window, that's the closest you've ever been to seeing black. You better run, cause there's a storm coming, there will be no snow, it will be black ice that will cut you deep and tear off your window pains. My name is not 0666914.

My name is 1564982. I'm white. I'm a woman. I speak sometimes. I can't anymore. The sins of my fathers are coming back. I don't even know who Cecil John Rhodes was. I'm colour-blind.

I was scared when the movement began; my privilege was exposed for the first time. My black friends weren't there anymore, they called me the enemy. I remember how they blocked everything and brought this institution to a standstill. I just wanted to go home. I couldn't. The same way my maid wears her doek with pride is the same way I wish I could carry my whiteness. But how? How can I be proud of being born into privilege, while my black neighbour, who used to call me friend doesn't speak to me anymore? I wish I could escape from this white pigment that I was born into, to be able to see my friends again.

The movement was meant to be about class not race. How do I protest when my voice is connected to the oppressive force that comes with being white? I could stand up and scream from the rooftops that say 'THESE FEELS WILL FALL', but will the friends I have lost say it back?

The female voice has never been respected, has it? I am a strong black woman named 6349874Y. Why is it that when the female body enters a space they are considered 'THE HELP'? The movement was never created by a man, but a woman with scars on her neck, trying to fix her vocal chords. Do you know her name or the pigment of her skin? She wasn't black, she wasn't white, she was the in-between. We didn't erect a statue for her that would honour what followed. Instead we placed two strong black men at the centrefold of every piece of writing and hashtag so that people would listen. The female voice had to be silenced; the female voice belongs at the end of the line handing out food parcels and being part of the background. I remember us strong black women. No. I remember us strong women wearing our doeks in solidarity, because the female voice was not heard during the movement, was it? We might have placed a strong black woman in-between the two strong black men but you tried to find her faults; you tried to prove that she wasn't strong enough. She was just another woman whose only role was to give birth.

Do you still not know the name of the woman who gave birth to the movement? She wasn't black, she wasn't white. She was woman. The female voice has never been respected. My name was 0862759; I left the institution a long time ago. I'm now an outsider looking in. I have a job, which is nice, I can finally afford certain things, I don't know how long that will last. I'm just patiently waiting for the NSFAS to knock on my door and take away everything that I have worked hard for. The students have spoken; I wish I spoke out sooner. I watch the news and see the pain that I went through, I was just surviving at the time and that was enough for me. These kids took their voices and said 'ENOUGH IS ENOUGH'. They took all the bullshit and threw it at the powers that be. They tried to fix the mistakes that we had made. We didn't fix anything when I was there, we just went through the motions so we could receive that piece of paper and stand on that stage and be told 'WELL DONE, YOU MADE IT'. I never considered anything beyond that day. I didn't think about the next generation of students and the struggles that they would face. I didn't think about my little sister who finishes matric this year. I was so concerned about me that I forgot my responsibility to her … so I'll silently … patiently wait for that knock on my door.

My name is 0708506j. White. Male. Privileged. I was born into a family that believed that the black face was less than human. I tried to escape that. My parents told me that Apartheid was just a means to an end. I told them that the white pigment we carry doesn't make us better than everyone else. I was 12 years old at the time; I found comfort from our domestic worker, Susan, a white name. I always called her Mam'Nomvula. That is who she was, she brought the rains that created a beautiful soul … she created my friend. I and he were connected by strings that I thought were detached from yesterday. I was wrong. I remember when family came over that would say 'CALL THE GARDEN BOY'. I always called him friend.

I would like to think that I'm colour-blind, but I know my friend is not. He was never called by his real name; he was always 'THE GARDEN BOY'. We would always write letters to each other when my parents weren't around. When the movement started we were both in our third year of Civil Engineering, we were both part of the movement. We tried to create a better world for both of us. I received a letter from him the day before we were meant to march to the Union Buildings, the letter read 'I'M GOING HOME FOR A FEW DAYS, WILL TALK TO YOU SOON'. He lied. He never went home with Mam'Nomvula.

On the day of the march to the Union Buildings I received a letter from Mam'Nomvula. I could hear her tears beyond the page. I never finished reading that letter. All I know is that on the 20th of October 2015, he took a taxi to Kliptown and shot himself. One bullet to the head. You wouldn't have heard about him because he wasn't 0708506j, he wasn't white, he wasn't privileged. They still call him garden boy ... I just miss my friend.

Dear 0708506j

I hope this letter finds you. This will be the last letter I send to you as I'm going away for a while, I'm not sure if I'll ever come back.

I'm a human being that feels the way that you do. I feel happy when the sun shines, the same way you do. I cry when the rain caresses my face before the storm comes. We bleed the same colours, but our colours are tainted, they are tarnished by the history that we never created. The nightmares have taken control of our dream, so we don't sleep anymore.

I'm not angry that you're white, I'm not ashamed that I'm black. I'm just worried about the story we would tell our children, will it be the same story that our parents told us. I'm not angry that you were told to be white, I'm not ashamed that I was told to be black. Do you remember the dreams we shared together? I and you standing on that stage, hand in hand, realising that we both had made it? I won't be able to stand on that stage with you anymore, they won't let me. You'll always be my friend. As I take my final sleep I hope you remember us, the way we wished our country could live up to the title of 'THE RAINBOW NATION'. When the movement ends, please tell them my story next to yours …

Your Dear Friend

Sithembiso 'Sthe Khali' Khalishwayo

Midnight in Lusikisiki
(or The Ruin of the Gentlewomen)
Sindiswa Busuku

One by one, the old womenfolk appear. Each falls to her knees in a field of mud. Floral pinafores flapping in the wind. Rain rolls down their faces and into their eyes. They are draped in black shawls. The trees above are creaking. They turn to look at each other. The field has turned to blood. They whisper into each other's hands, 'Cover me with a veil. Evening has collapsed.' After a long silence, they climb to their feet. Then the womenfolk begin to walk backwards. A fluorescent swarm of fireflies rises agile in the sky. Each woman scatters in a separate direction. Each disappears into the tall reeds. All of them waving and smiling so broadly their lips begin to crack. The field has turned to bone.

Soon they begin to laugh uncontrollably through their tears and their blood-stained teeth, whispering, 'Lonmin has hollowed out our aching bodies.'

Crowd Gathered, Salivating for a Taste of Blood
Sihle Ntuli

violence,
as a pain
shared between men,

it has been said
time and time again,
to be a man
one must save face
at all times,

it was pain
that drove defence
against a loss of power,

to think how clenched fist
was once a symbol of power
down the road
to grievous bodily harm,

now a symbol
of how man will hold onto the pain
never letting go.

Letsatsi
Maneo Mohale

In your mother's red golf, you ask her what benoni means.
Son of my sorrow – hearing the sun instead,
you turn the word over in your mind like a coin.

Ghosts are living in mine dumps
as your mother drives you home. Honeycomb
mountains are brittle. Tomorrow, you ask

her for a crunchie after school. Like all names
of the bible, benoni sounds ancient. Out
your mother's mouth magic. Manjink. Meijik.

You are still small enough to hide
inside the good book's rice paper pages. You do not know yet,
what you are – have not had leviticus angled at you

like an ice-pick. For now, the bible is a hand drum
for women dressed in white and blue. Ko katlehong,
in a pockmarked garage, they are women made of clouds

and ocean. They make terrifying sea-wide music. Sgubhu:
the plastic bottom of everything that has a heart. Shells
and bottletops on ankles. How neatly

old and new gods sit together.
In school, you meet a man called cecil john
and learn the word *pioneer*.

Turn the word over in your mind like a coin.
Your mother is a witness. Your mother is
a pioneer, not yet knocking on doors

to tell people about the good news.
You wonder if cecil was a witness too, wonder
on whose doors he knocked,

for which god, to spread what good news.

Blvcksuburbia
Anga Mamfanya

I've often heard of beauty
Virtue, narrated by men and women well beyond youth
Matured and refined like red wine
Their stories carved into the wrinkled lines of their foreheads
Their facial expressions burdened with chapters of lives lived in full
They recall memories from the memoirs written on their scars
The elders, they claim to know you

You, with your nationwide smile and heart made of gold
The rhythm in the blues of your skin
Jazz hands and saxophones at the bottom of your throat
It's you who calms the liquor in a man's breath
And forges his fists into hands that know how to pray
You who reminds dark pigment where home is
More than just 4 walls and creaky floorboards
Modest houses and narrow streets that become soccer fields in
    the evenings
Just before the sun breaks into a thousand stars and pigeon-toed
    dreams
Lay themselves bare on the pavement and pay homage to you
Dreams that mend broken bones and straighten bent spines and
    crooked smiles
Made of rusty barbed wire
Dreams dreamt in caged minds
Tamed lion cubs with question marks bouncing off trampoline
    tongues

What happens when happiness is rendered hollow by gunshots
    fired into the night's skin?

What happens when men abuse women like politicians abuse
  wealth?
Men who stopped being men a very long time ago
Men who sit outside with tobacco pipe in hand and smoke rising
In speechless protest as it fills the lungs of youth
Who will learn to put out forest fires in a single breath
Violence is not the answer until it is
Hector will tell you that it is the language of the unheard
How else are we expected to retaliate when our spirits rage war
Inside of our chests and words no longer have the will to fight
  through clenched teeth?

Can you hear the revolution coming?
It is closer than it's ever been
Slaves are refusing to eat crumbs off the master's table
Women are assuming their roles at the forefront of change
And deadbeat dads are returning home after seeing themselves
Through the eyes of their unborn children
A revolution is coming
Like the pregnant belly of a teenage mother
Or rain upon arid land
Sweet suburbia, not even polluted skies could taint your beauty
Your virtue narrated by a zealous youth.
Newfound hope birthed into the land.
A story retold.

History in my Body
Uhuru Phalafala

I

'Burying Seeds'
After Ama Codjoe

History in my body,
a history of personalities
and lords of war
dominant in muscle memory.
History that turns the tide
of centuries-old violence
against us, the unspoken and unsung.
I write this history.
residing in my body.
It resounds yours too.
In speaking of widows and wives of history
we speak to ourselves.
When it dies a violent death,
as it often does, history returns
to wives and grandmothers.
And children too,
protected by the water of their mothers' bodies.
We are those children,
and, like water, we remember.
History's tide swells within us in full moon,
during the constant endings and beginnings
of our bodies remaking themselves.
With blood.
Every month.

Blood that separates us
from our fathers and brothers
in the mosque.
We sing its name:
our foremothers' refrain.

II

'Black women likely to suffer
From severe uterine fibroids'
Medical reasons unknown!
Speculation cites
diet, weight, alcohol
Even hair relaxers and shampoo

Colonial sexual warfare
Is not suspected
Systemic rape
And terror of invasion
Are not cited

High infant mortality rate,
Swallowing and entombing
Grief, loss, and mourning,
Burying children and husbands
In cemeteries of our bodies
Don't make the list

White boot to pregnant stomach
Gynecological experiments
Historical insemination
Forced sterilisation

High maternal death risk
Natal and post-natal neglect
Are not culprits

Our bodies are voids
In which history
Casts its shameful acts
Our bodies are vaults
storing trauma that still breathes.
In.our.wombs

The ocean seeks revenge
Sibongile Fisher

What licks at death like the common tongue brushing against
    headlines?
A woman in South Africa
Or her son in the US of A?
What bites at their fate like bad teeth born on the wrong side
    of the tracks?
A black man
A white man
Or, the unprefixed reality that men are landmines buried beneath
    the lust of power
And the rest of us have to walk this earth trying to avoid them
But we can't unmother them, unlove them, unfriend them
So we make humans of monsters
Make lovers of fraudsters
Make friends of swindlers
Until death gropes us with their hands
Then we are enraged
Pull the ocean over our eyes
And seek revenge

But here, the ocean is not heard
Not seen for anything else outside its beauty
A home for the living
A home for the spirits
The genesis that broke the lands and gave it life.

When will it end?
The breathing in the coffins

The loving in the mortuaries
The caring in the horror films

The ocean seeks revenge

fatigue of revolution
Masai Sepuru

I am tired of this old machine that runs on coal, blood, and steam
My knuckles are bloody from banging against its steel
I feel as though I have wasted my life away, navigating these streets
With a map passed down by those that came before me
Trying to find a way out of this labyrinth of bright corridors and dark alleys
Is this all that my art is for?
Protest and reiterate what has already been said before
There must be more, surely

I also want to write poems about roses and lilies
Protest for climate change, and endangered species
But how?
When my kind is also endangered
Constantly in danger, or seen as a danger
So much anger
So much healing needed
There isn't enough skin for these inherited wounds
Still, the machine finds a way to curve in new ones

Sometimes I get tired of playing the victim
Only to be reminded that I am not playing at all
Even though my life is treated as a game
Points for political gain
Companies use black rage to promote sales
When regardless of all the lives at stake
Politicians and the media still debate my life for argument's sake

Semantics and nuances
Time wasted
Justice delayed
Pit us against each other
'Whose shade is more deserving?'
'Who is more African'
'Who kneels for which god?'
'Who identifies as what?'
Movement derailed
When the smoke clears and the dust settles
It is all still the same

But all we ever asked for is to be seen as people
Not just fuel
Not just ones and zeroes
Or gears and levers that run the machine
But people
Regardless of our shapes and form

I am tired of sounding like the crazy one
The conspiracy theorist
'Here he goes again with his black history shit'
My resistance is met with resistance
Despite the evidence
Documentaries and libraries filled with the history of my
    people's tragedy spread across centuries
I find myself protesting against the same enemy
It is tiring, draining my energy

Am I a joke to you?
It is a joke now to be woke
A meme

A way to mock my struggle
I am always told to get over it,
And sometimes I think I should
I guess it's my fault for thinking they will page through the books
And my words would be the ones to finally break through

How naïve
To claim to be tired
When all I have done is shared a few posts
Read a few quotes
Cast a few votes
Wrote a few poems
And poked a few holes
And to think that I will be the one to finally sink this boat?

This machine
It reached my shores long before I was born
Who am I to think that I will sink it?
When it threw Hani overboard
And made Biko walk the plank
Took Sobukwe to an island
And turned Nelson into its friend
And instead of returning the land, it made us sign papers
    and shake hands

But its engine is still running, the turbines are still turning
I am overwhelmed by the sheer size of it
Its history of murdering my people fills me with rage and
    justifies my cowardice
I look back with admiration and shame at the youth before me
How they looked deep in its eyes and dared to burn it
And I dare to say that I am tired?

Baldwin was tired
Ali was tired
Bra Hugh was tired
Mama Winnie was tired
And they have earned their rest
I am only getting started

Index of poems

#FeesMustFall   144

Africa: My Native Land   25
Always a Suspect   43

Because I'm Black   40
Black Beauty   120
from: black trial   71
Blvcksuburbia   156
born(e) to the grave   121

Citizen Minus   130
'Civilised' Labour Policy   26
clots of blood   118
Crowd Gathered, Salivating for a Taste of Blood   153
Custodian of our Spirit   107

Death   86
Dying Ground, The   69

fatigue of revolution   163
Forgotten, The   146

Freedom's Child   36

Getting off the Ride   55
Gold Mines, The   30

History in my body   158

In this World, my Sister   96

john 1:1 and me   115
jol'iinkomo   124

Kneel and Pray   47

Letsatsi   154
Location Fires   52
Love poem for the 'Problematic' Black Womxn, A   133

Making of a Servant, The   27
Man of Smoke, The   48
Midnight in Lusikisiki (or The Ruin of the Gentlewomen)   152
Miners, The   45
morning caught me, the   67
My Name   104

Ngwana wa Azania   91
Nineteen Seventy-Six   90

ocean seeks revenge, The   161
Old Homes   83
Our Immortal Mother   84

Pension Jiveass, The   44

Question, The   78

Riot Policeman, A   110

Soul's Disparity   82

thinking about a white christmas   68

Untitled poem #1   139

We the Dancers   105
What's in this Black 'Shit'   53
Wooden Spoon   109

Your Poem Saved Me   138

Index of poets

Abrahams, Peter 36

Banoobhai, Shabbir 67
Bhengu, Zéwande Bk. 144
Billie, Ayanda 138
Busuku, Sindiswa 152

Davids, Jennifer 52
Dhlomo, HIE 40
Dube, AC 25

Fisher, Sibongile 161

Gantsho, Vangile 118

Heeger, Khadija 130

Johennesse, Fhazel 68
Jolobe, JJR 27

Khalishwayo, Sithembiso ('Sthe Khali') 146
Kunene, Ashanti 139

Langa, Mandlenkosi 44
Lange Stewart, Puleng 133
Lebakeng, Monnapule 69
LR 26

Maahlamela, David wa 124
Madingoane, Ingoapele 71
Mamfanya, Anga 156
Masango, Lebohang 115
Mbuli, Mafika 45
Miya, Themba ka 78
Mmutle, Molahlehi wa 84
Mnyayiza, Nkathazo ka 47
Mogotsi, Motlase 82
Mohale, Maneo 154
Moja-Mphuso, David 83
Mokhele, Siza Nkosi 140
Mphahlele, Es'kia 86
Msimang, Mjele 121
Mthimkulu, Oupa Thando 90
Mtshali, Mbuyiseni Oswald 43
Mutloatse, Mothobi 91

Ndebele, Njabulo S 48
Ntuli, Sihle 153

Phalafala, Uhuru 158
Phalanndwa, Nthambeleni 96

Selepe, Magoleng wa 104
Sepuru, Masai 163
Serote, Mongane Wally 53

Shoro, Katleho Kano   120
Skeef, Eugene   105
Stemmet, Farouk   107

van Wyk, Christopher   110
Vilakazi, BW   30

Zwide, K   109